MW00989265

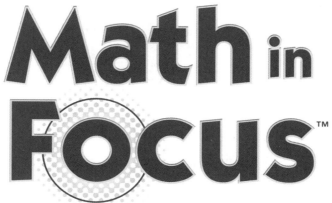

Math in Focus™

The Singapore Approach

Assessments

1

Author
Zalina A. Jalil

Marshall Cavendish Education

Great Source®
HOUGHTON MIFFLIN HARCOURT
Supplemental Publishers

Published by Marshall Cavendish Education
An imprint of Marshall Cavendish International (Singapore) Private Limited
A member of Times Publishing Limited

Marshall Cavendish International (Singapore) Private Limited
Times Centre, 1 New Industrial Road
Singapore 536196
Tel: +65 6411 0820
Fax: +65 6266 3677
E-mail: fps@sg.marshallcavendish.com
Website: www.marshallcavendish.com/education

Distributed by
Great Source
A division of Houghton Mifflin Harcourt Publishing Company
181 Ballardvale Street
P.O. Box 7050
Wilmington, MA 01887-7050
Tel: 1-800-289-4490
Website: www.greatsource.com

First published 2009
Reprinted 2010 (twice)

Math in Focus Assessments 1
ISBN 978-0-669-01599-7

Printed in Singapore

3 4 5 6 7 8 1897 16 15 14 13 12 11 10
4500262591 B C D E

Contents

Introducing

Math in Focus

Assessments

Assessments 1 is written to complement *Math in Focus™: The Singapore Approach* Grade 1.

Assessments 1 provides both a pretest and a chapter test for each chapter of the Student Books, as well as two Benchmark Assessments, a Mid-Year Test, and an End-of-Year Test. Chapter tests are in test-prep format with a multiple-choice section and an open response section to help students become familiar and comfortable with formal assessment situations. Word problems and non-routine problems included throughout the tests provide important problem-solving practice.

BLANK

Name: ______________________________ Date: ________________

PRE-TEST 1 Numbers to 10

Concepts and Skills

Count.

Match the 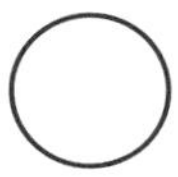 to the  to show the same number.

1.

2.

3.

4.

5.

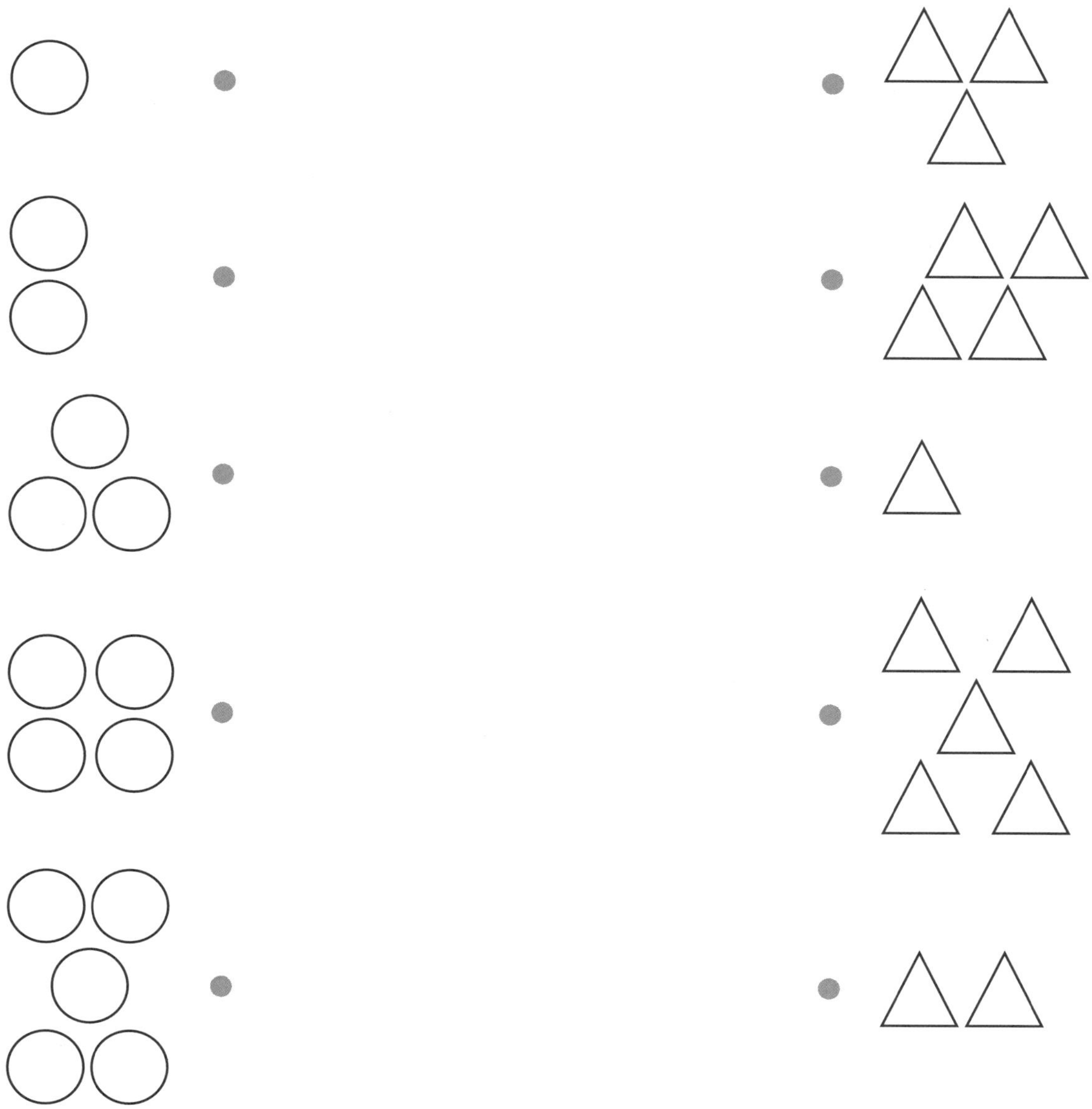

Name: ______________________ Date: ______________

TEST PREP

1 Numbers to 10

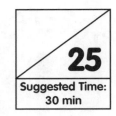

25
Suggested Time: 30 min

Multiple Choice

(5 x 2 points = 10 points)

Fill in the circle next to the correct answer.

1. Count.

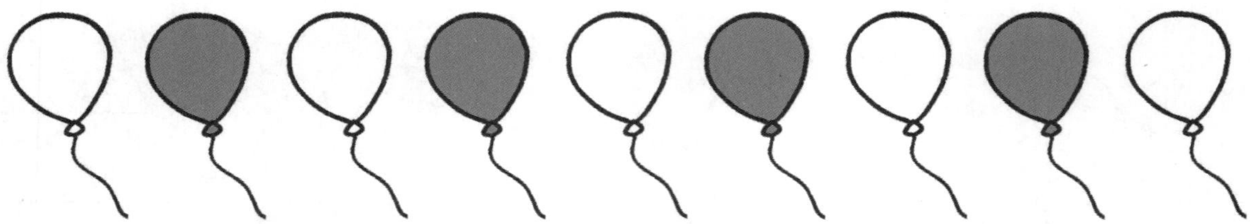

Ⓐ 6 Ⓑ 7 Ⓒ 9 Ⓓ 10

2. Count.

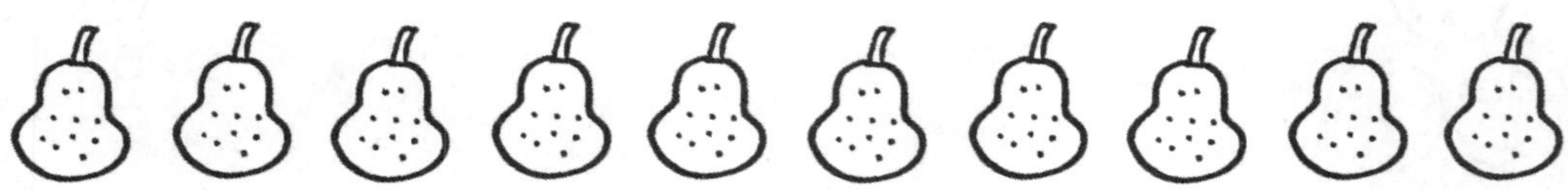

Ⓐ zero Ⓑ three Ⓒ five Ⓓ ten

3. What number comes next in the pattern?

4	5	6	7	?

Ⓐ 10 Ⓑ 8 Ⓒ 3 Ⓓ 0

Name: ______________________ Date: ______________

4. I want 1 more flower. How many flowers will there be then?

(A) 1 (B) 4 (C) 5 (D) 6

5. Which number is less than 6?

(A) 3 (B) 6 (C) 7 (D) 9

Short Answer

(5 x 2 points = 10 points)

Follow the directions.

6. Write the number in the box.

zero	

Name: ______________________ Date: ______________

7. Count.
Then write the number in words.

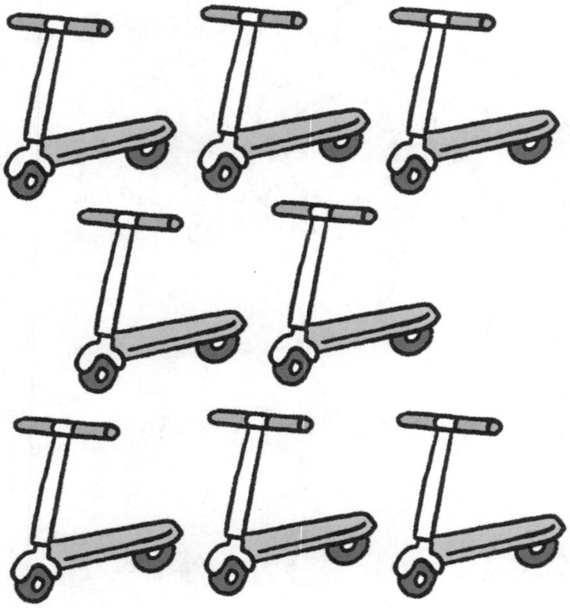

There are ______________  .

Name: ______________________ Date: ______________

8. Color the two groups that have the same number of fruits.

9. Circle the group with more.

10. Complete the number pattern.

	9	8		6		4

Name: ____________________ Date: ____________

Extended Response

(5 x 1 point = 5 points)

Solve.
Fill in the blanks with *the same, more,* or *fewer.*

Emily, Pat, Amy, and Sheree have some bracelets.

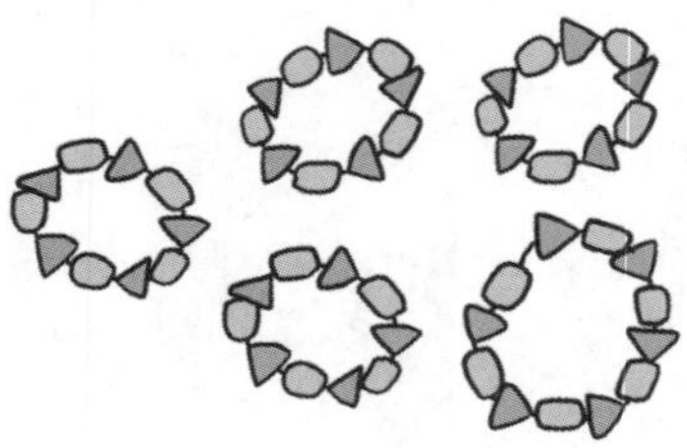

Amy

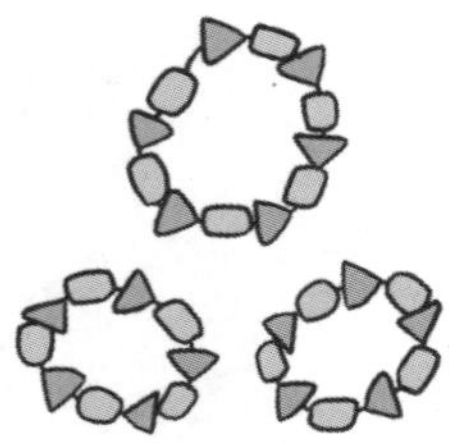

Pat

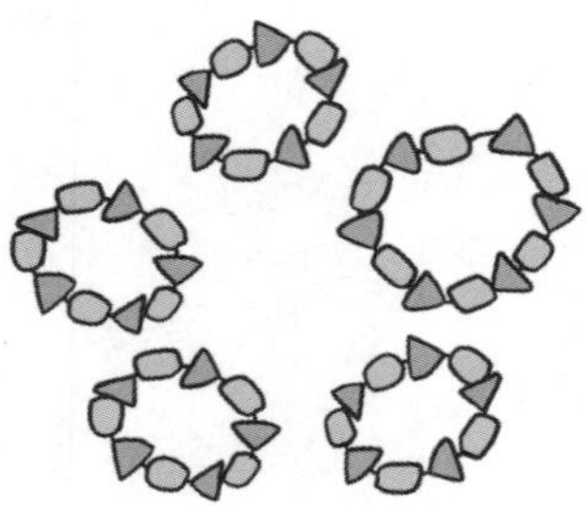

Emily

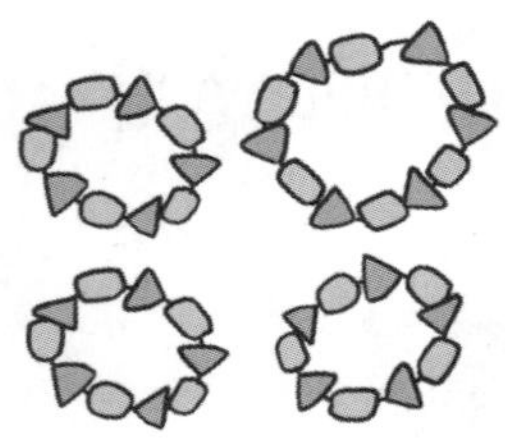

Sheree

11. Sheree has ____________ bracelets than Pat.

12. Amy and Emily have ____________ number of bracelets.

13. Sheree has ____________ bracelets than Amy.

Write any three numbers.

14. less than 5: ______ ______ ______

15. more than 6: ______ ______ ______

Name: ______________________ Date: ______________

PRE-TEST 2 Number Bonds

Vocabulary

Match the pictures to the number.

1.  • • (10)

2. 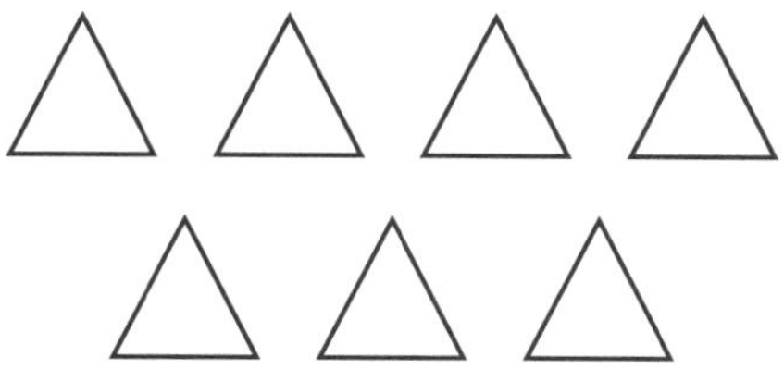 • • (6)

3. 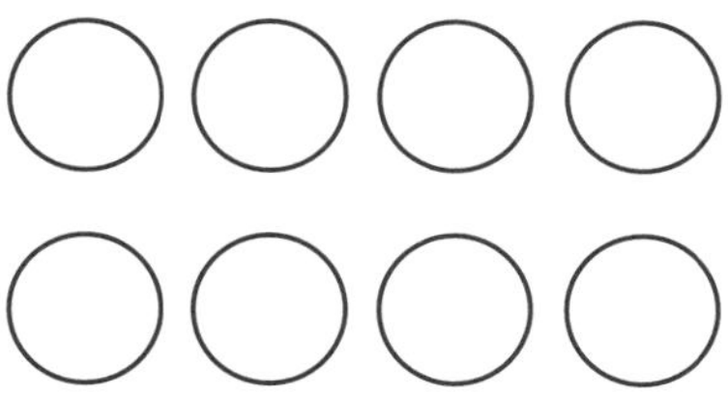 • • (9)

4. 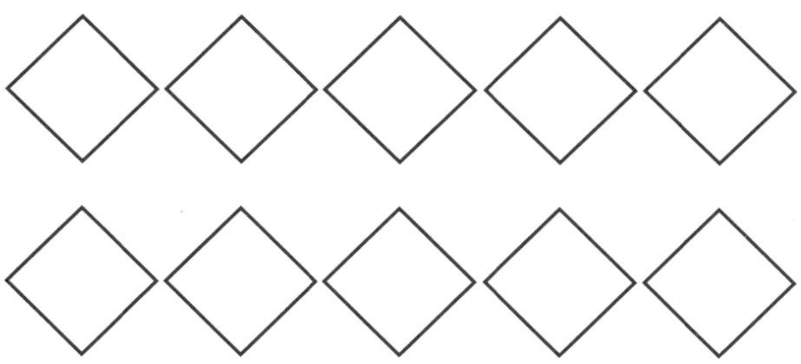 • • (7)

5. 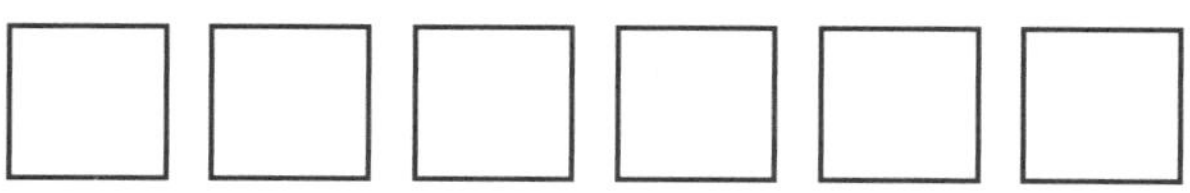 • • (8)

Name: ______________________ Date: ______________

Concepts and Skills

Fill in the blanks.

6. 1 more than 8 is ______.

7. 1 less than 5 is ______.

8. ______ is 1 more than 3.

9. ______ is 1 less than 6.

Problem Solving

Draw 1 more dot.
Then fill in the missing numbers.

10. 1 more than 0 is ______.

11. 1 more than 1 is ______. ●

12. 1 more than 2 is ______. ● ●

13. 1 more than 3 is ______. ● ● ●

14. 1 more than 4 is ______. ● ● ● ●

Name: ______________________ Date: ______________

15. 1 more than 5 is ______.

16. 1 more than 6 is ______.

17. 1 more than 7 is ______.

18. 1 more than 8 is ______.

19. 1 more than 9 is ______.

Name: ______________________ Date: ______________

TEST PREP 2 Number Bonds

25

Suggested Time: 30 min

Multiple Choice

(5 x 2 points = 10 points)

Fill in the circle next to the correct answer.

1.

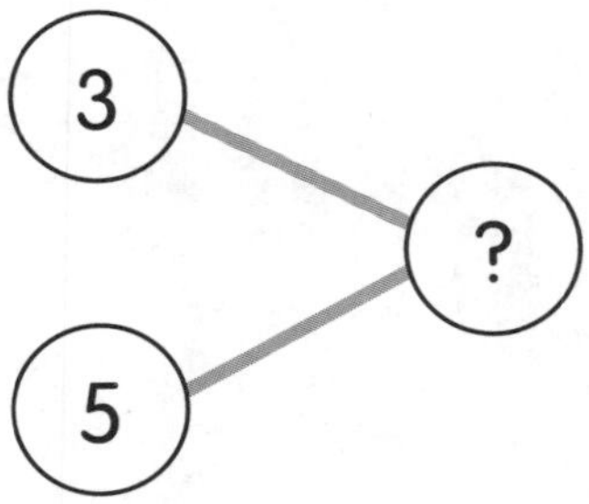

What is the missing number?

Ⓐ 2 Ⓑ 3 Ⓒ 5 Ⓓ 8

2. 3 and ☐ make 7.

What is the missing number?

Ⓐ 2 Ⓑ 3 Ⓒ 4 Ⓓ 5

3. How many more whales must you draw to show 9 whales?

Ⓐ 3 Ⓑ 4 Ⓒ 5 Ⓓ 6

Name: ______________________ Date: ______________

4.

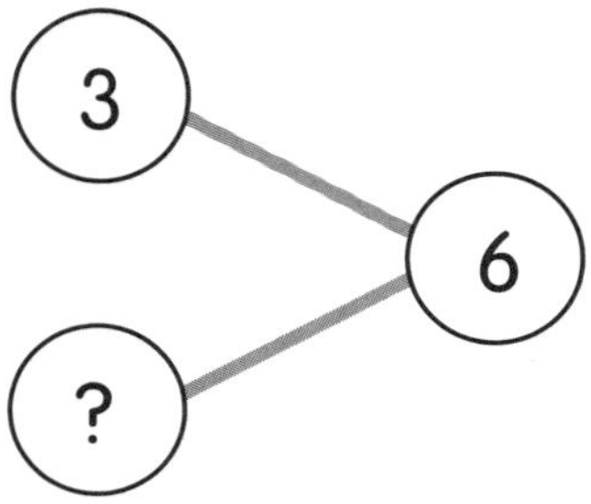

What is the missing number?

Ⓐ 0 Ⓑ 3 Ⓒ 5 Ⓓ 9

5. Look at the number bonds.

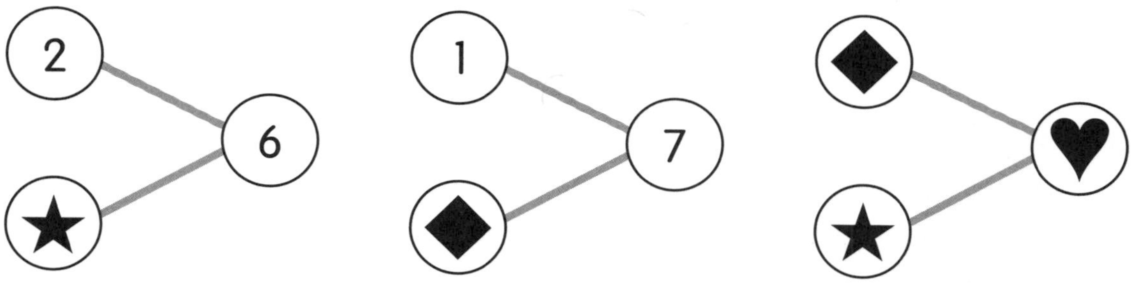

What is ♥?

Ⓐ 4 Ⓑ 6 Ⓒ 7 Ⓓ 10

Name: ______________________ Date: ____________

Short Answer

(5 x 2 points = 10 points)

Follow the directions.

6. Look at the picture.
Complete the number bond.

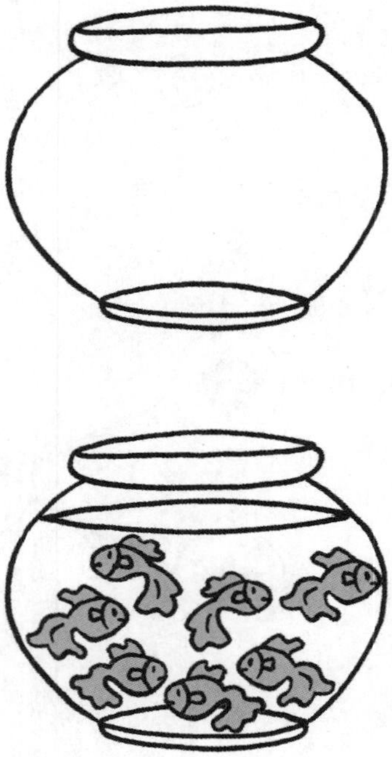

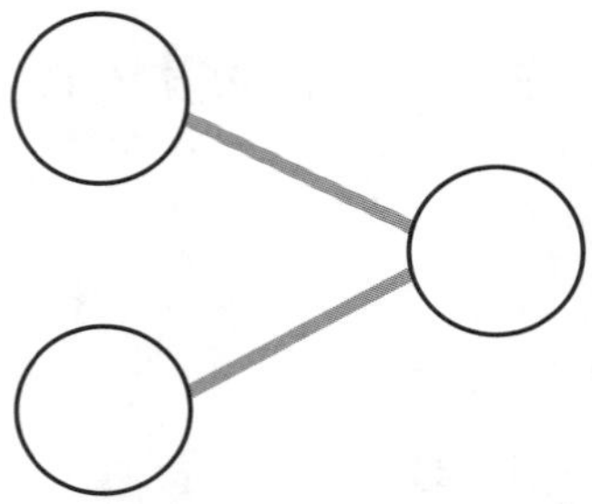

7. Circle two numbers that make 9.

2 3 5 6 8

Name: ______________________ Date: ______________

8. Fill in the missing number.

5 and ______ make 8.

9. Complete the number bond with three numbers from the box.

3	9	4
7	2	

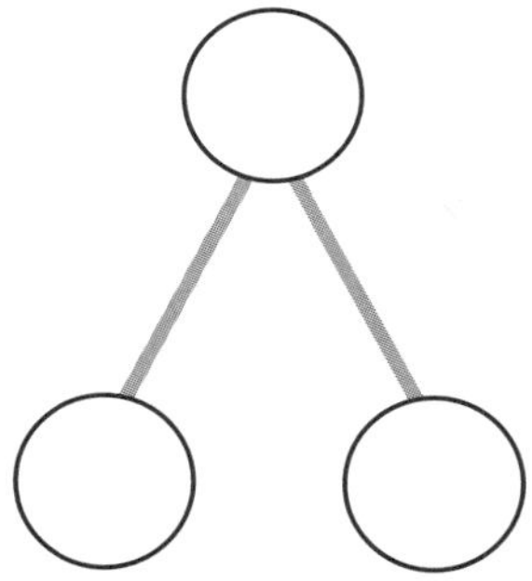

10. Complete the number bond.

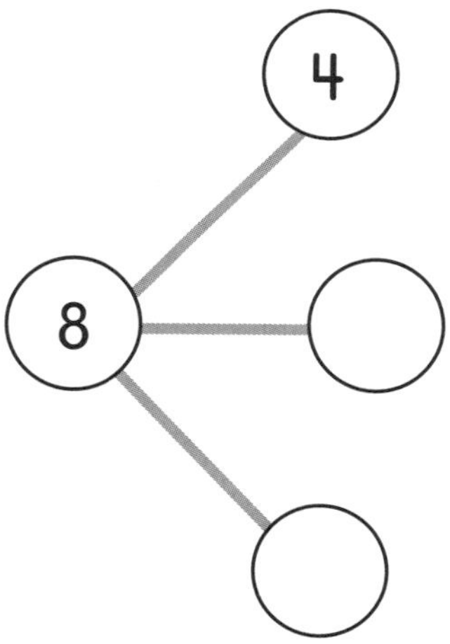

Name: ______________________ Date: ______________

Extended Response (5 points)

Complete the number bonds.

11.

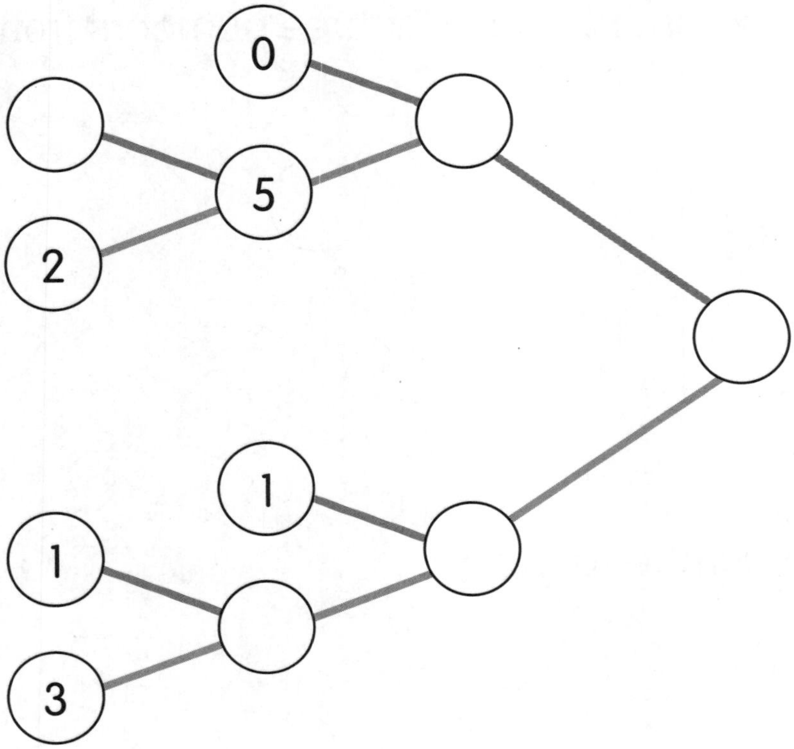

Name: ________________________ Date: ________________

PRE-TEST 3 Addition Facts to 10

Vocabulary

Fill in the blanks.
Use the words in the box.

less than
make
more than

1. 3 is __________ 7.

2. 1 __________ 2 is 3.

3. 8 is 1 __________ 9.

4. 4 and 6 __________ 10.

Concepts and Skills

Fill in the blanks.

5. 1 more than 9 is ______.

6. 1 less than 2 is ______.

7. ______ is 1 less than 7.

8. ______ is 1 more than 7.

Name: ______________________ Date: ____________

Problem Solving

Complete the number bonds.

9. 3 and 6 make 9.
What other number bonds can you use to make 9?
Make all the other number bonds for 9.

Example

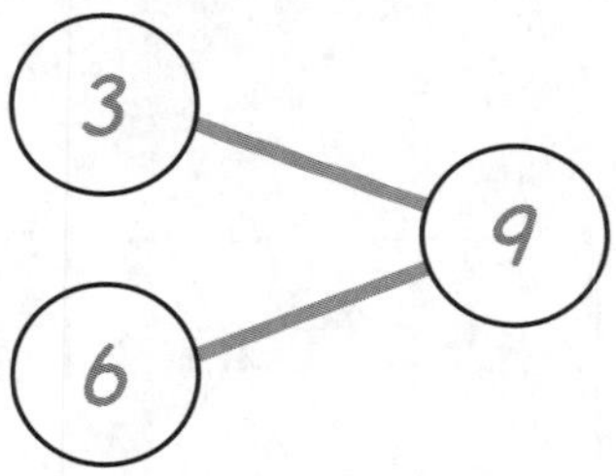

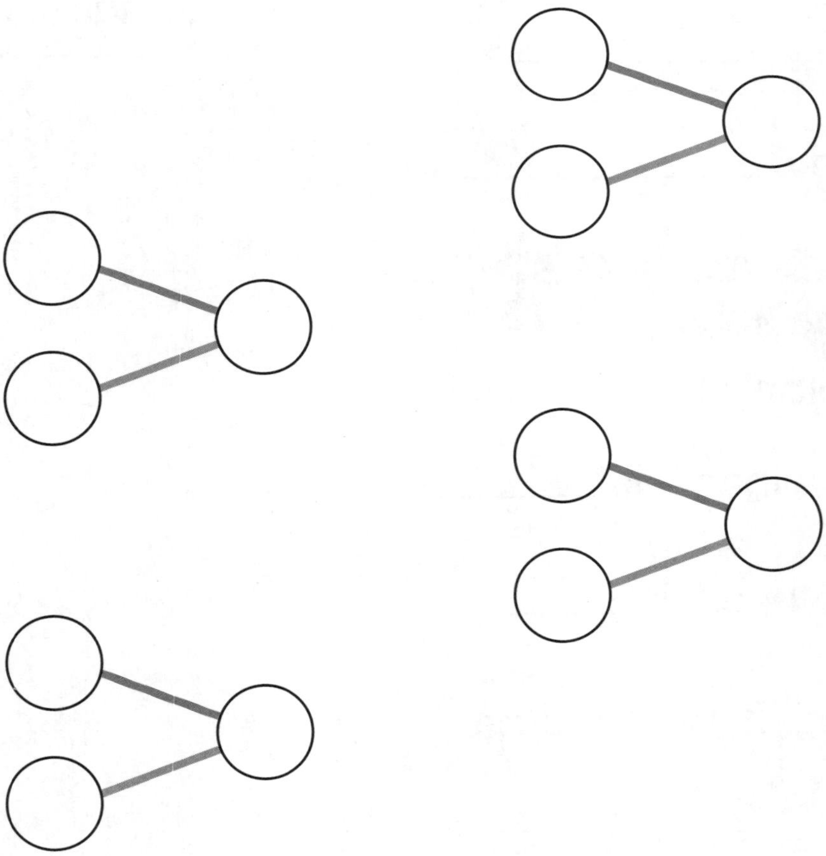

Name: ____________________ Date: ____________

TEST PREP 3 Addition Facts to 10

25

Suggested Time: 30 min

Multiple Choice (5 x 2 points = 10 points)

Fill in the circle next to the correct answer.

1. How many circles and triangles are there in all?

Ⓐ 3 + 5 Ⓑ 3 + 6 Ⓒ 6 + 2 Ⓓ 7 + 3

2. What is 3 + 3?

Ⓐ 0 Ⓑ 3 Ⓒ 6 Ⓓ 8

3. What is 3 + 4?

Ⓐ 4 Ⓑ 6 Ⓒ 7 Ⓓ 9

4. What is 8 more than 2?

Ⓐ 4 Ⓑ 6 Ⓒ 8 Ⓓ 10

Name: ______________________________ Date: ______________

5. Four bells are in the box.
How many bells are there in all?

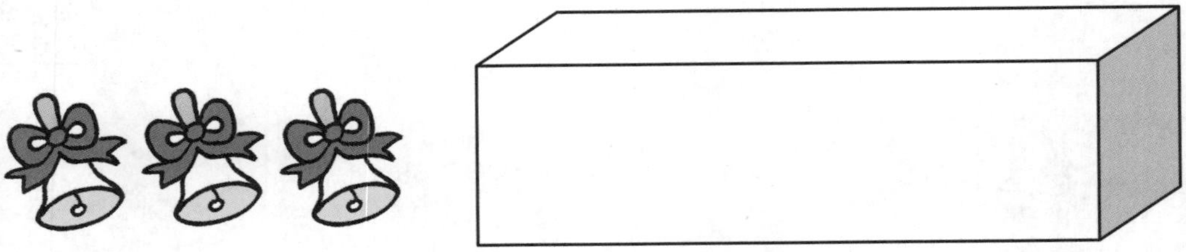

Ⓐ 4 Ⓑ 6 Ⓒ 7 Ⓓ 10

Short Answer

(5 x 2 points = 10 points)

Follow the directions.

6. Count.
Then write the numbers in the boxes.

☐ + ☐ = ☐

7. Complete the number bond.
Then write an addition sentence.

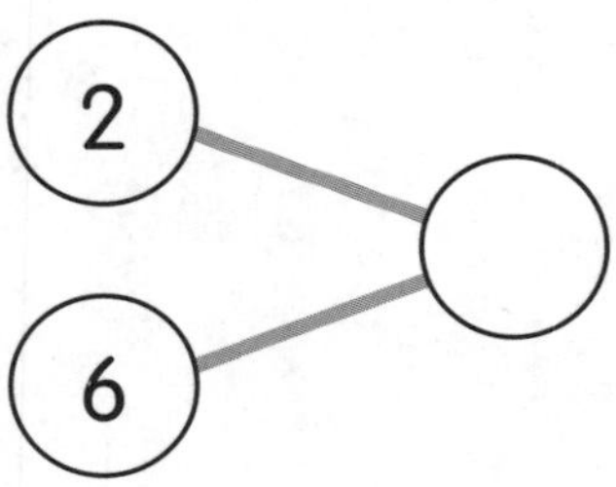

☐ ○ ☐ = ☐

Name: ______________________ Date: ______________

8. Color the flower that gives the number in the box.

6

9. Jolene has 6 big bows and 4 small bows.
How many bows does she have in all?

She has ______ bows in all.

10. Write a number sentence using the following:

9	6	3	=	+

____

Extended Response

(Question 11: 2 points, Question 12: 3 points)

Solve.
Show your work.

11. Wendy has some hats.
5 hats have stars on them.
2 hats do not have stars on them.
How many hats does Wendy have in all?

☐ ◯ ☐ = ☐

Wendy has ______ hats in all.

Name: ______________________ Date: ____________

12. How many pieces of fruit are there in all?

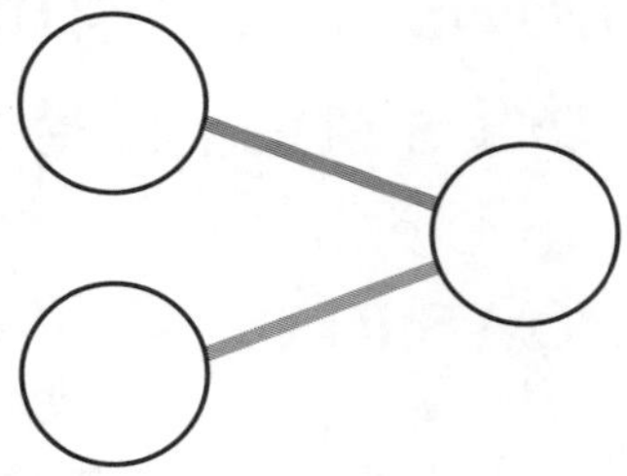

$\square + \square = \square$

There are ______ pieces of fruit in all.

Name: ______________________ Date: ______________

PRE-TEST 4 Subtraction Facts to 10

Vocabulary

Fill in the blanks.
Use the words in the box.

1. 7 is ______________ 5.

2. 6 is ______________ 9.

3. 3 + 4 is ______________ 7.

4. 9 is 1 ______________ 10.

equal to
less than
more than

Concepts and Skills

Fill in the blanks.

5. 1 less than 5 is ______.

6. ______ is 1 less than 6.

7. 4 and ______ make 9.

8. ______ and 0 make 8.

Name: ______________________ Date: ______________

Problem Solving

Complete the number bonds.

9. 5 and 5 make 10.
What other number bonds can you use to make 10?
Make all the other number bonds for 10.

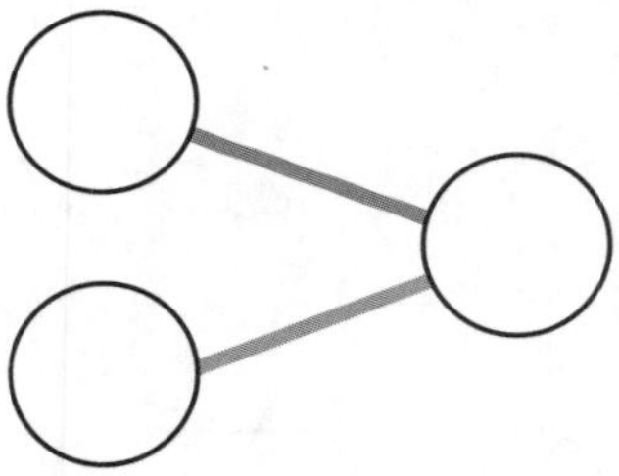

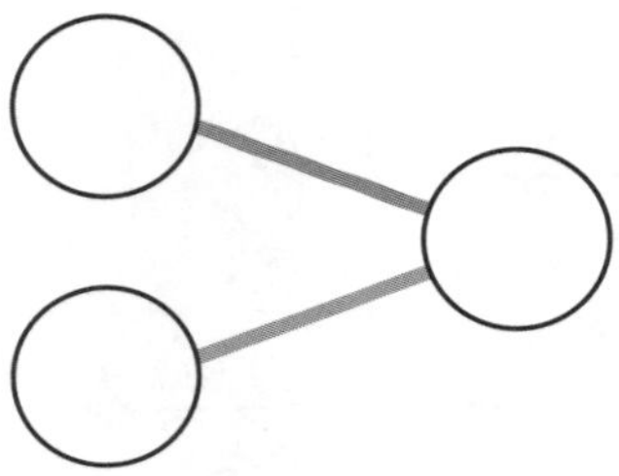

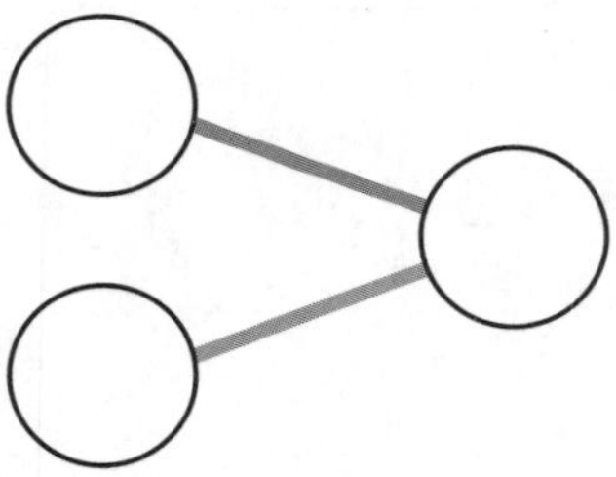

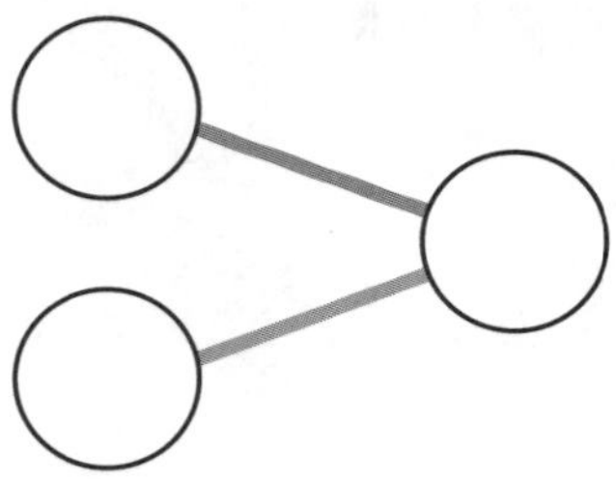

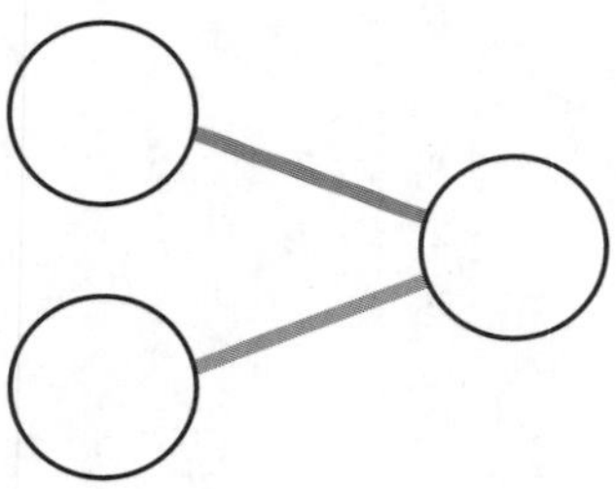

Name: ______________________ Date: ______________

TEST PREP 4 Subtraction Facts to 10

25

Suggested Time: 30 min

Multiple Choice

(5 x 2 points = 10 points)

Fill in the circle next to the correct answer.

1. What is 3 less than 7?

Ⓐ 10 Ⓑ 7 Ⓒ 4 Ⓓ 3

2. Look at the number bond.

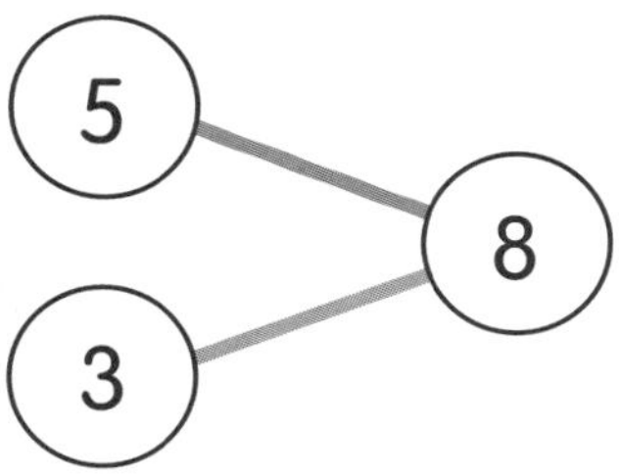

Which is **not** correct?

Ⓐ 3 + 5 = 8

Ⓑ 3 + 8 = 5

Ⓒ 8 − 3 = 5

Ⓓ 8 − 5 = 3

Name: ______________________ Date: ____________

3. Nick has 8 apples.
He gives 5 apples away.
How many apples does Nick have left?

Ⓐ 13 Ⓑ 8 Ⓒ 5 Ⓓ 3

4. Bob has 7 buttons.
Pam has 2 fewer buttons than Bob.
How many buttons does Pam have?

Ⓐ 2 Ⓑ 5 Ⓒ 7 Ⓓ 9

5. What is the same as 3 + 5?

Ⓐ 5 – 1 Ⓑ 7 – 1 Ⓒ 8 – 1 Ⓓ 9 – 1

Short Answer

(5 x 2 points = 10 points)

Follow the directions.

6. Subtract.

9 – 3 = ______

Name: ____________________ Date: ____________

7. Look at the picture.
Write a subtraction sentence.

☐ ◯ ☐ = ☐

8. Fill in the blank.

______ – 2 = 3

9. Cross out 3 balls.
Then write the missing number.

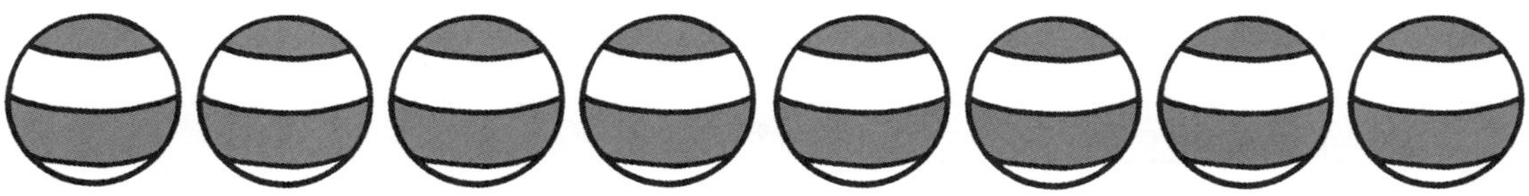

3 less than 8 is ______.

10. Fill in the blank.

10 – 5 = 7 – ______

Name: ____________________ Date: ____________

Extended Response

(Question 11: 2 points, Question 12: 3 points)

Solve.
Show your work.

11. Peter buys 9 fish.
He gives 3 fish away.
How many fish does Peter have left?

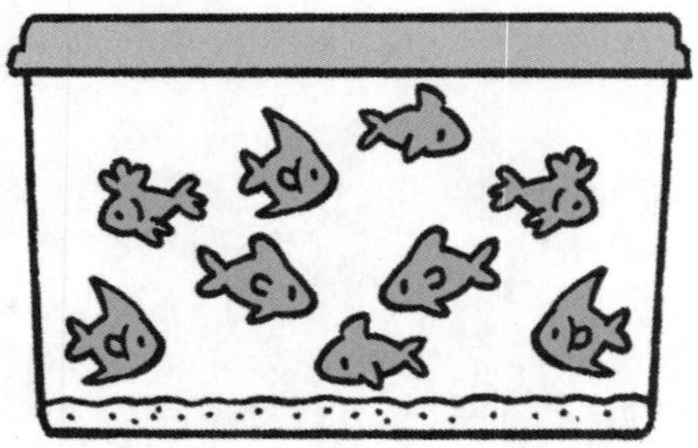

☐ ◯ ☐ = ☐

Peter has ______ fish left.

Name: ____________________ Date: ____________

12. Mrs. Lee buys some muffins.
Her family eats 6 muffins.
Mrs. Lee has 3 muffins left.
How many muffins did she have at first?

$\square - 6 = 3$

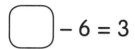

$6 + 3 = \square$ is the related addition fact.

She had ______ muffins at first.

Name: ______________________ Date: ______________

Benchmark Assessment 1
for Chapters 1 to 4

/ 50
Suggested Time: 45 min

Multiple Choice
(10 x 2 points = 20 points)

Fill in the circle next to the correct answer.

1. What comes just after 9?

Ⓐ 6 Ⓑ 7 Ⓒ 8 Ⓓ 10

2. The numbers are arranged in a pattern.
They are in order, beginning with the least.

What is the missing number?

Ⓐ 2 Ⓑ 5 Ⓒ 8 Ⓓ 4

3. Which of these numbers is greater than 4 but less than 7?

Ⓐ 3 Ⓑ 6 Ⓒ 8 Ⓓ 9

Name: ______________________ Date: ______________

4. Look at the number bond.

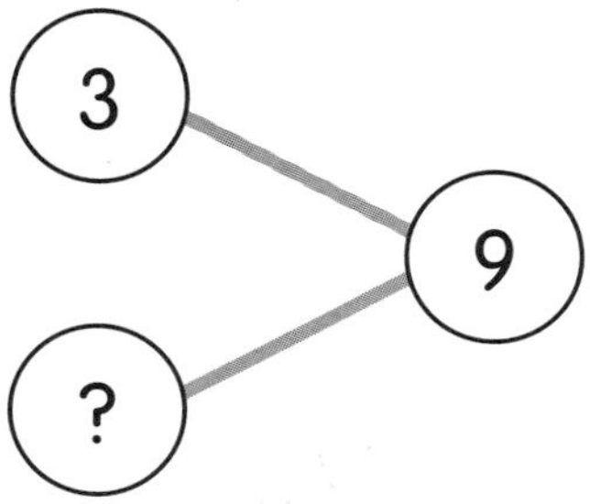

What is the missing number?

Ⓐ 3 Ⓑ 6 Ⓒ 7 Ⓓ 8

5. Look at the number bond.

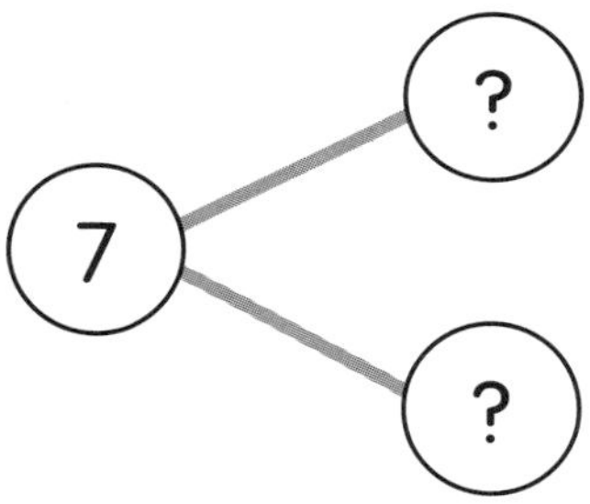

What are the missing numbers?

Ⓐ 2 and 4 Ⓑ 2 and 5 Ⓒ 3 and 5 Ⓓ 3 and 6

6. Which of these gives 8?

Ⓐ 3 + 4 Ⓑ 2 + 6 Ⓒ 5 + 1 Ⓓ 1 + 2 + 3

Name: ______________________________ Date: ______________

7. David has 3 more strawberries than Susan.

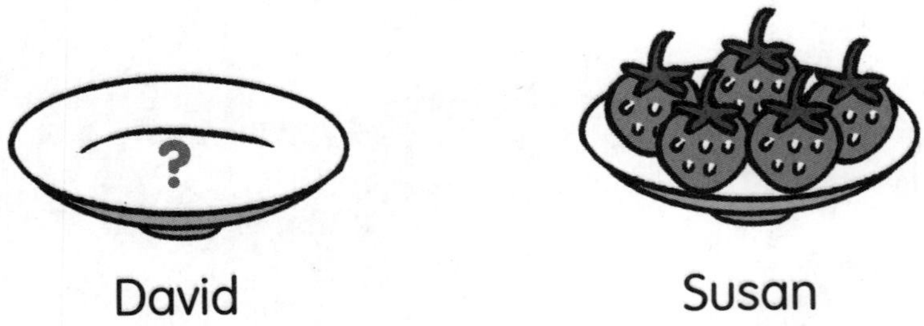

How many strawberries does David have?

Ⓐ 3 Ⓑ 5 Ⓒ 8 Ⓓ 9

8. Which of these is equal to 8?

Ⓐ 9 – 3 Ⓑ 3 + 6 Ⓒ 9 – 1 Ⓓ 2 + 7

9. 8 – ☐ = 2 + 6

What is the missing number?

Ⓐ 1 Ⓑ 2 Ⓒ 3 Ⓓ 0

10. Steve puts 6 pears in a box.
Mary takes 2 pears out of the box.
How many pears are left in the box?

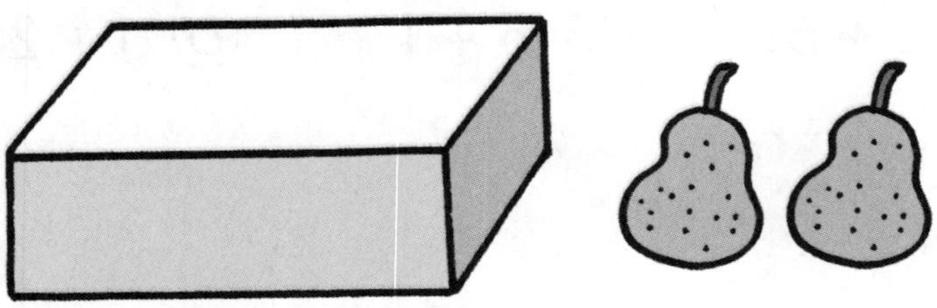

Ⓐ 2 Ⓑ 3 Ⓒ 4 Ⓓ 5

Name: ______________________________ Date: ______________

Short Answer

(10 x 2 points = 20 points)

Follow the directions.

11. Count and write the number in words.

______________ stars

12. Circle the correct number of objects.

13. Check (✔) the set that has fewer objects.

Name: ____________________ Date: ____________

14. Complete the number pattern.

0		2	3

15. Make two different number bonds for 10.

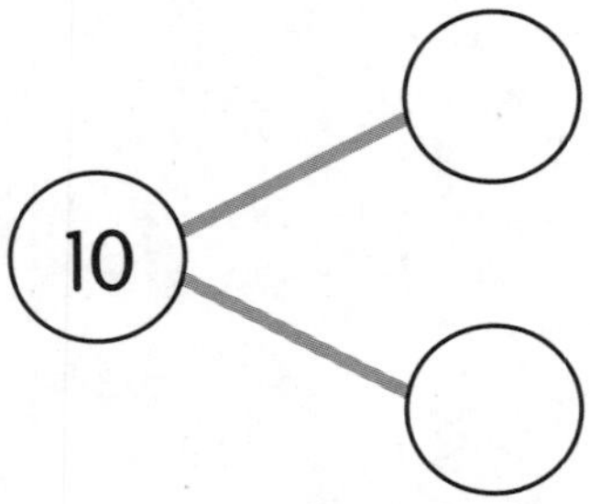

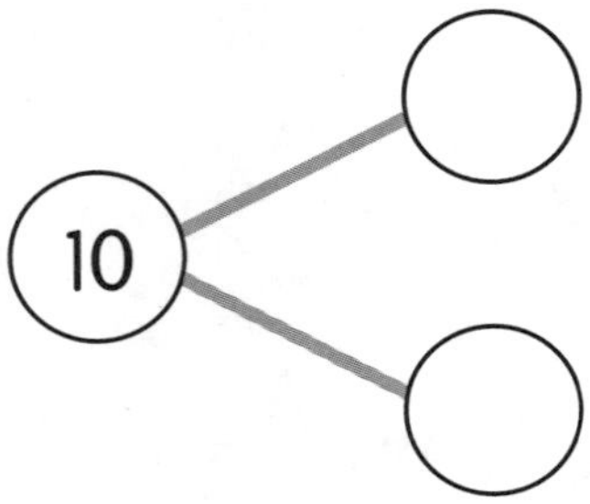

16. Look at the picture.
Complete the number bond.
Then fill in the blanks.

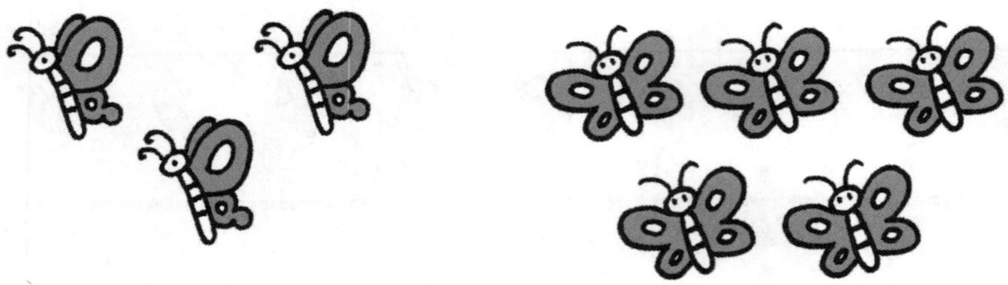

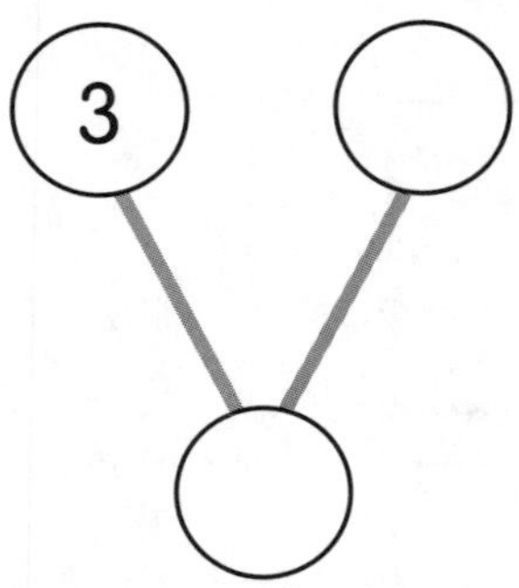

3 + ______ = ______

Name: ____________________ Date: ____________

17. Write the missing number.

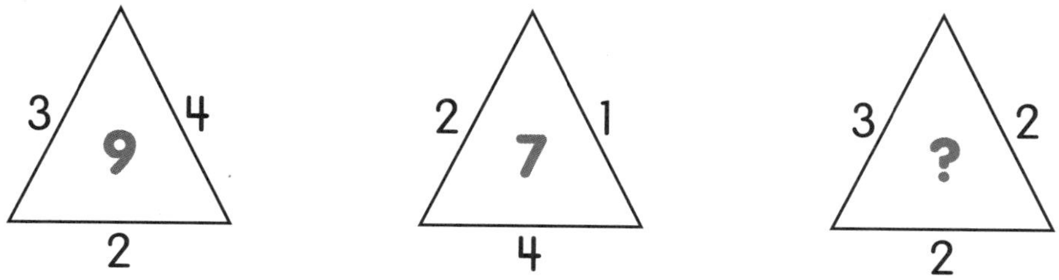

______

18. Color the picture that gives the answer 4.

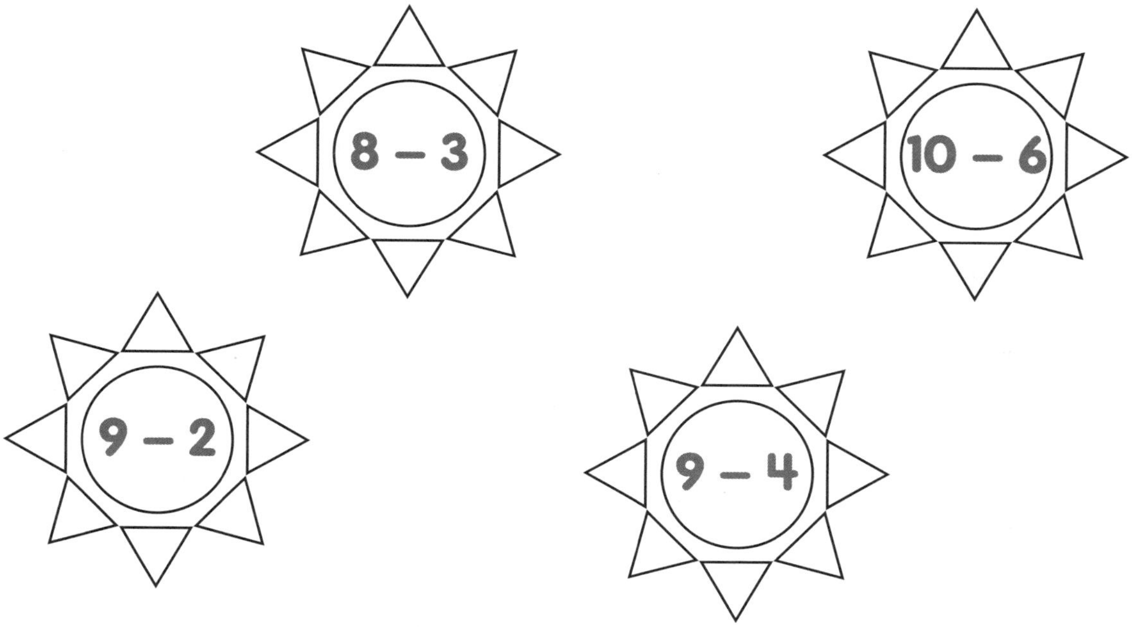

19. Fill in the blank.

______ + 5 = 9 – 2

Name: ______________________ Date: ____________

20. Fill in the blank.

☆ − 2 = 8

☆ − ◗ = 4

Then ◗ = ______.

Extended Response

(Questions 21 and 22: 2 x 3 points = 6 points, Question 23: 4 points)

Solve.
Show your work.

21. Michael has 4 books.
Sharon gives him 3 more books.
How many books does Michael have now?

☐ ◯ ☐ = ☐

Michael has ______ books now.

Name: ______________________ Date: ______________

22. Jada has 5 crackers.
Will eats 1 of her crackers.
How many crackers does Jada have now?

☐ ◯ ☐ = ☐

Jada has ______ crackers now.

23. John has 5 big shells
He finds 4 small shells.
He gives 2 shells away.
How many shells does John have left?

☐ ◯ ☐ = ☐

John had ______ shells.

☐ ◯ ☐ = ☐

John has ______ shells left.

Name: ____________________ Date: ____________

Bonus Questions

Follow the directions.

1. Fill in the ◯ with numbers 1 to 6.

Each ◯—◯—◯ adds up to 10.

Use each number only once.

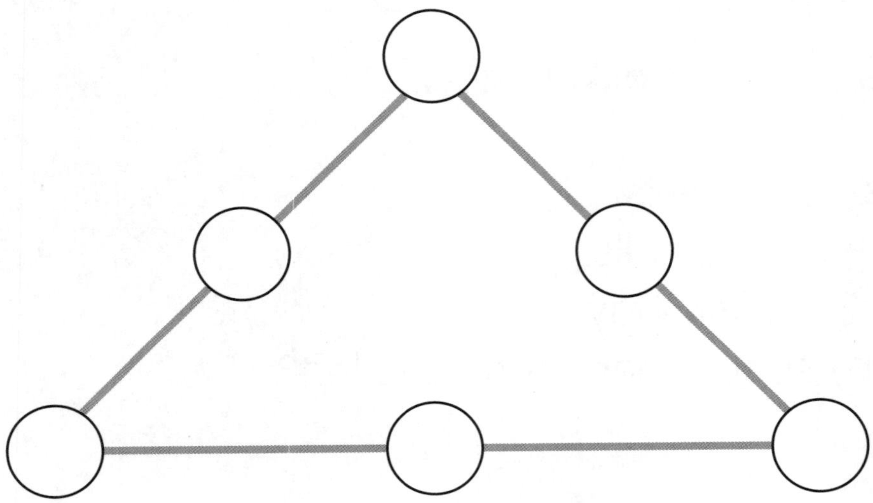

Name: ______________________ Date: ____________

2. What numbers do ◆ and ♥ stand for?
Write the numbers.

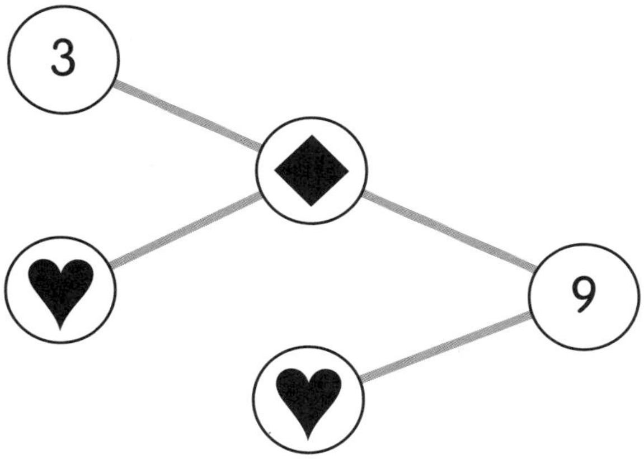

◆ = ☐ ♥ = ☐

3. Look at the pattern.
Fill in the missing numbers.

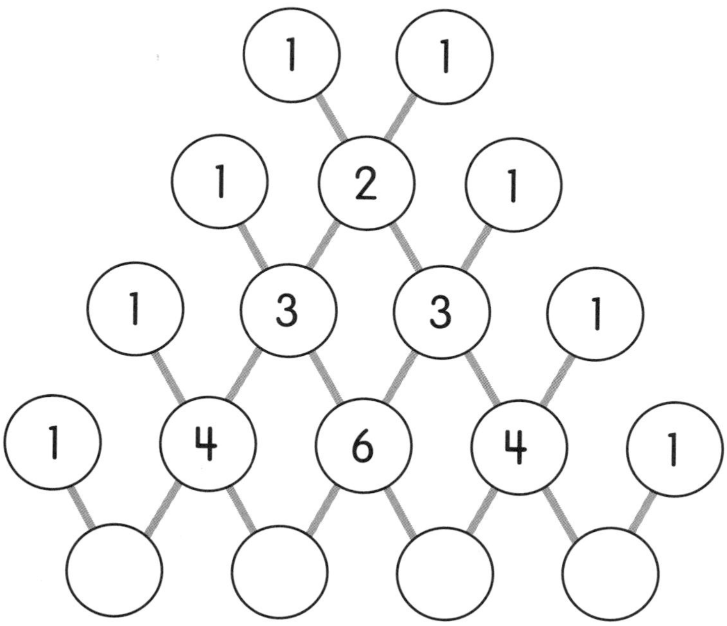

Name: ______________________ Date: ______________

PRE-TEST 5

Shapes and Patterns

Vocabulary

Match the shapes to the names.

1.	 •	• rectangle
2.	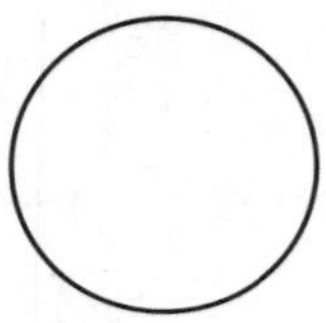 •	• square
3.	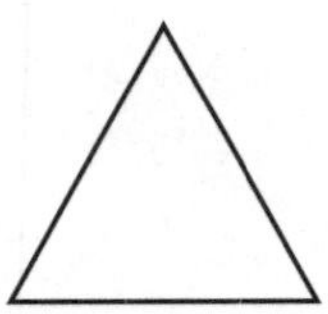 •	• circle
4.	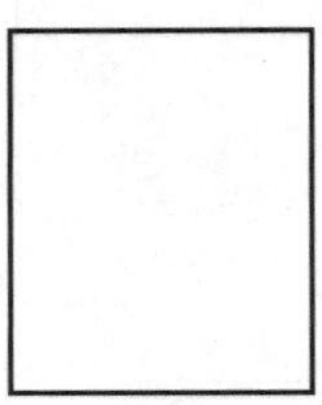 •	• triangle

Name: ______________________ Date: ______________

Concepts and Skills

Circle the shapes that match the things.

5.

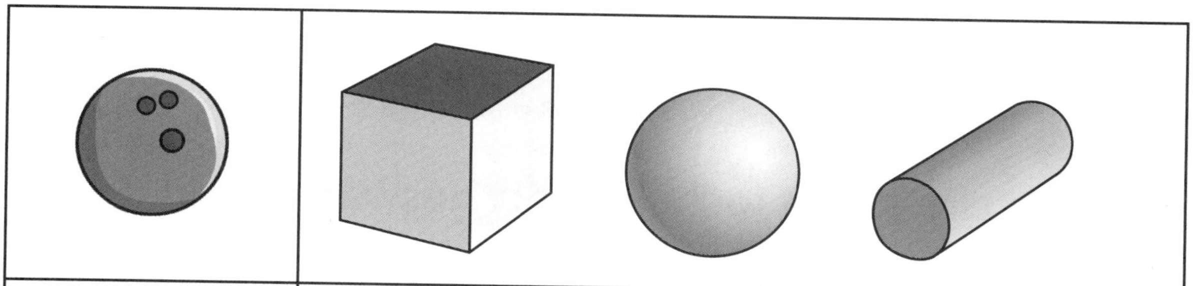

6.

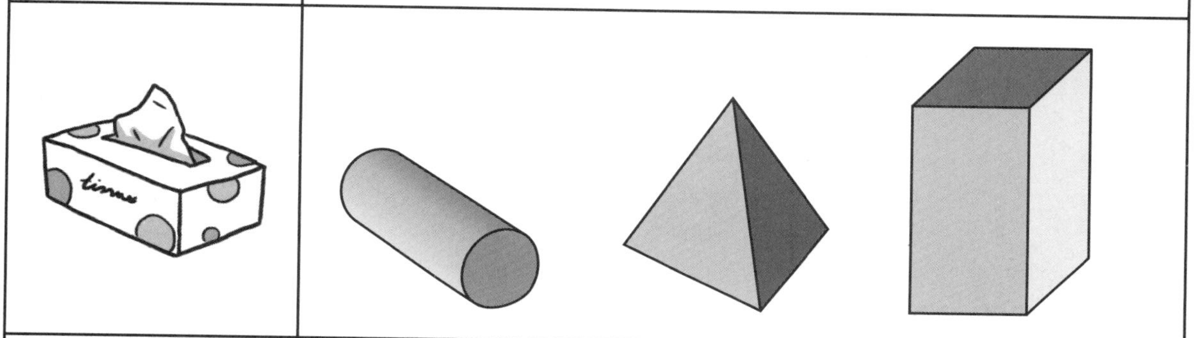

7.

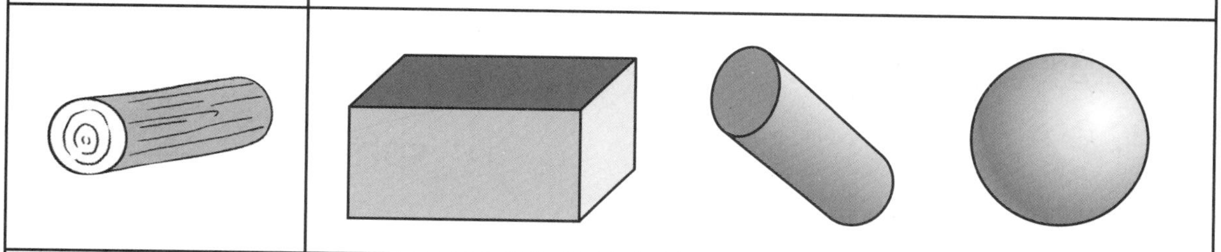

8.

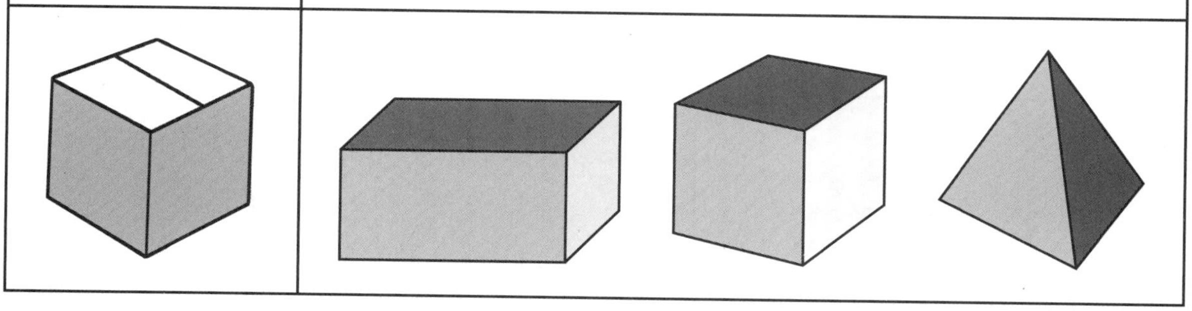

Name: ______________________ Date: ______________

TEST PREP

5 Shapes and Patterns

	25
Suggested Time: 30 min	

Multiple Choice

(5 x 2 points = 10 points)

Fill in the circle next to the correct answer.

1.

What shape is the hat?

Ⓐ cylinder Ⓑ cube

Ⓒ cone Ⓓ sphere

2. Look at the picture.

Which shape is **not** in the picture?

Ⓐ square Ⓑ rectangle

Ⓒ circle Ⓓ triangle

Name: ____________________ Date: ____________

3. Which thing has the shape of a rectangle?

Ⓐ 

Ⓑ 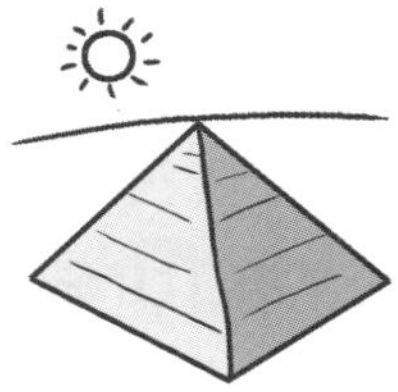

Ⓒ 

Ⓓ 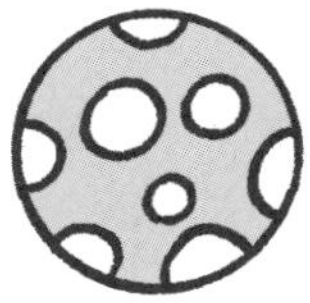

4. Which set of shapes are of the same shape but different size?

Ⓐ 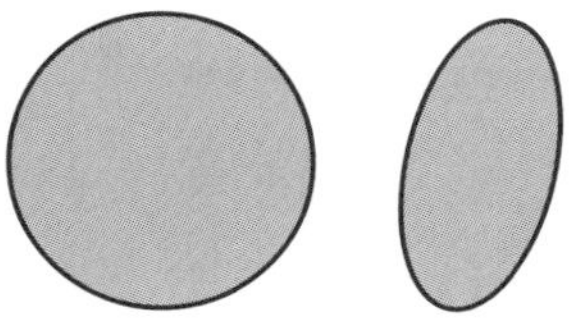

Ⓑ 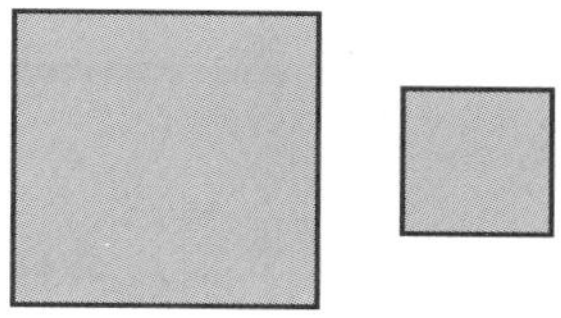

Ⓒ 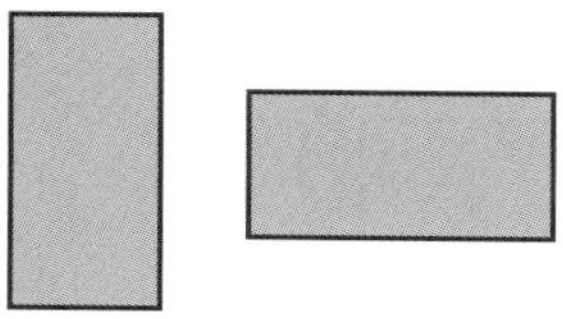

Ⓓ 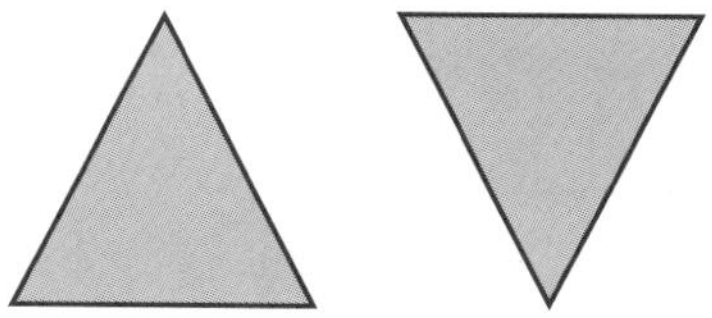

5. Which shape has three sides?

Ⓐ 

Ⓑ 

Ⓒ 

Ⓓ 

Name: ______________________ Date: ____________

Short Answer

(5 x 2 points = 10 points)

Follow the directions.

6. Look at the picture.
Color the smaller triangle.

7. Color two shapes that can form a square.

8. Name the shape of the shaded part.

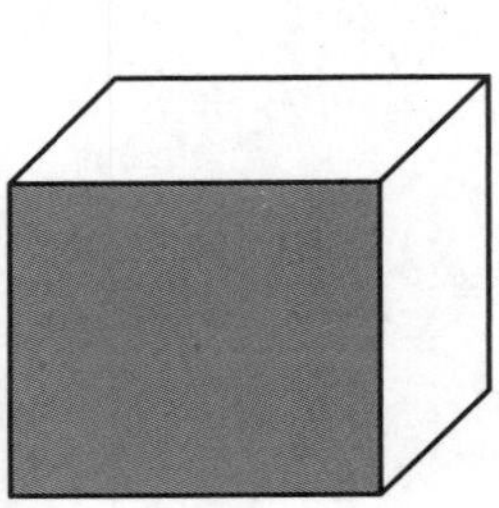

____

rectangle
square

Name: ______________________ Date: ______________

9. What comes next?
Draw the next shape in the box.

10. What comes next?
Color the correct shape.

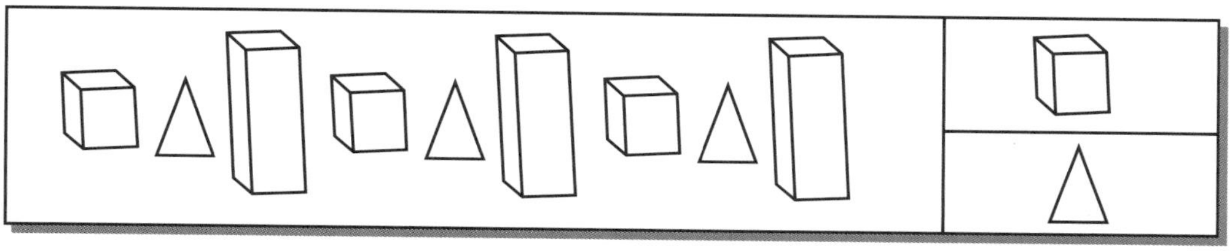

Extended Response

(Question 11: 2 points, Questions 12 to 14: 3 x 1 point = 3 points)

Solve.
Show your work.

11. Circle the things that can roll.

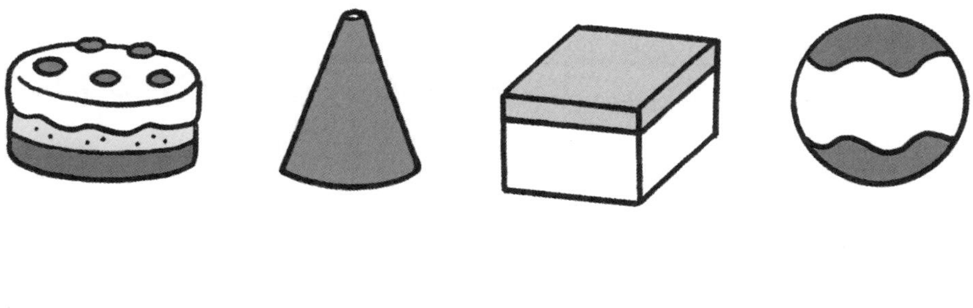

Name: ______________________ Date: ______________

Look at the picture.
Fill in the blanks.

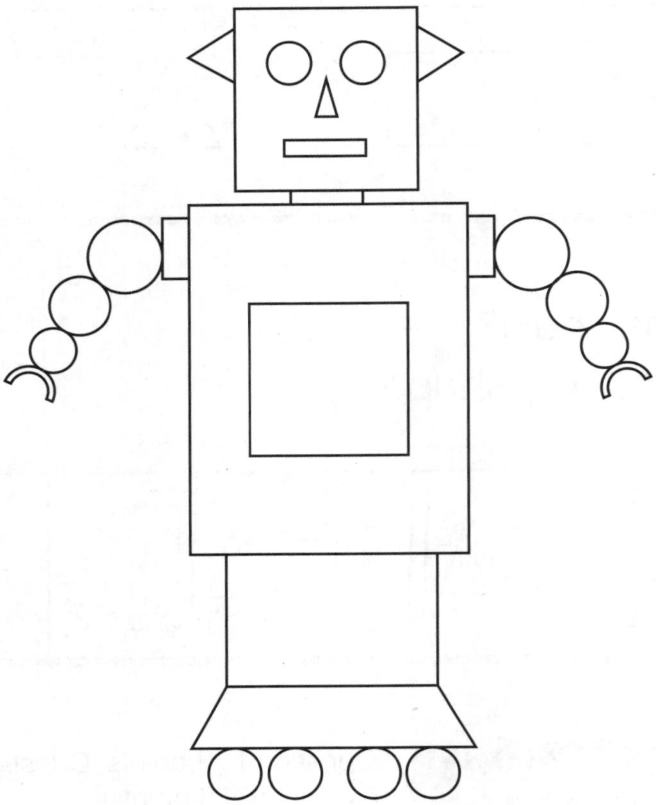

12. The picture has ______ triangles.

13. The picture has ______ rectangles.

14. The picture has ______ more rectangles than squares.

Name: ______________________ Date: ______________

PRE-TEST 6

Ordinal Numbers and Position

Vocabulary

Match.

1. 

• • third

2. 

• • first

3. 

• • second

Name: ______________________ Date: ______________

Concepts and Skills

Look at these letters.
Fill in the blanks.

A B C D E F G H I J

1st

4. The first letter is ______.

5. The last letter is ______.

6. The 3rd letter is ______.

7. The letter after the third letter is ______.

8. The letter before the last letter is ______.

Name: ______________________ Date: ______________

Problem Solving

Who is the person who comes in first in a race? Write the letters in the boxes.

9. The second letter in 'two' [ ]

10. The second letter in 'five' [ ]

11. The 1st letter in 'nine' [ ]

12. The last letter in 'ten' [ ]

13. The 3rd letter in 'one' [ ]

14. The last letter in 'four' [ ]

Name: ______________________ Date: ______________

TEST PREP 6

Ordinal Numbers and Position

25

Suggested Time: 30 min

Multiple Choice

(5 x 2 points = 10 points)

Fill in the circle next to the correct answer.

1. Look at the picture.
What is Peter Pan's position from the left?

Cinderella Snow White Pinnochio Peter Pan

Ⓐ 1st Ⓑ 2nd Ⓒ 3rd Ⓓ 4th

2. Look at the picture.

Roy is ☐ Ivan and Nathan.

James Ivan Roy Nathan

What is the missing word?

Ⓐ before Ⓑ after Ⓒ between Ⓓ behind

Name: ______________________________ Date: ________________

3. What shape is second from the right?

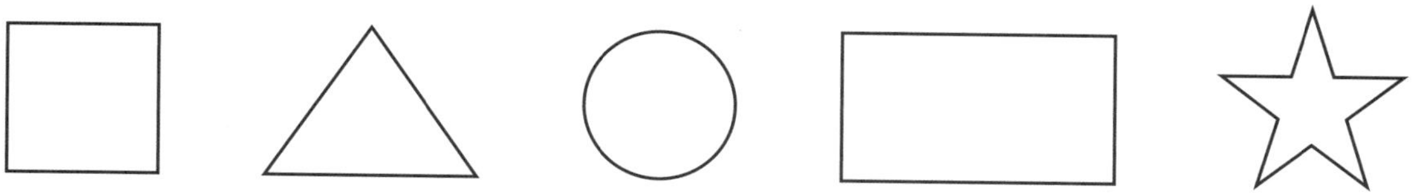

Ⓐ square Ⓑ triangle

Ⓒ circle Ⓓ rectangle

4. In which picture is the circle to the left of the square?

Ⓐ 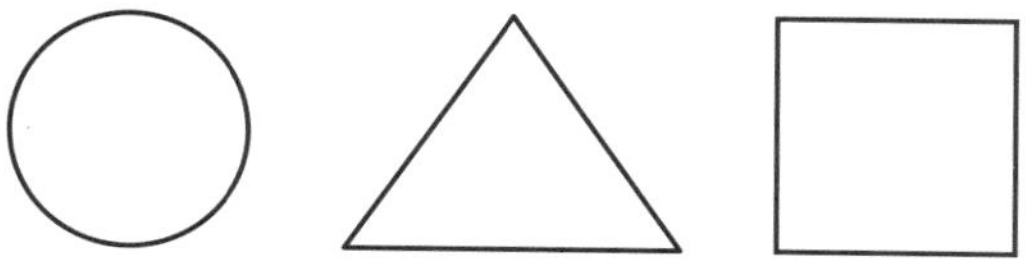

Ⓑ 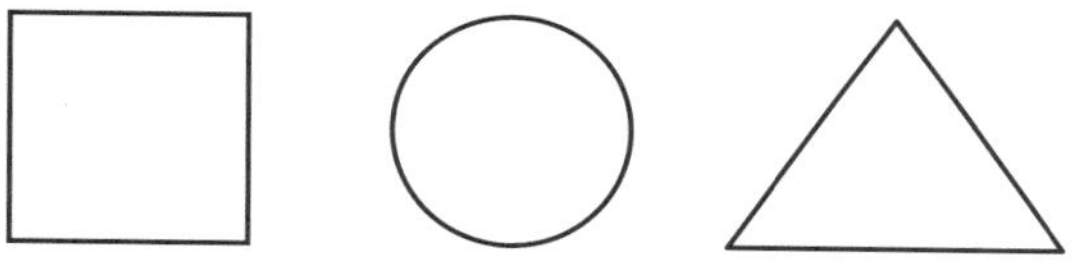

Ⓒ 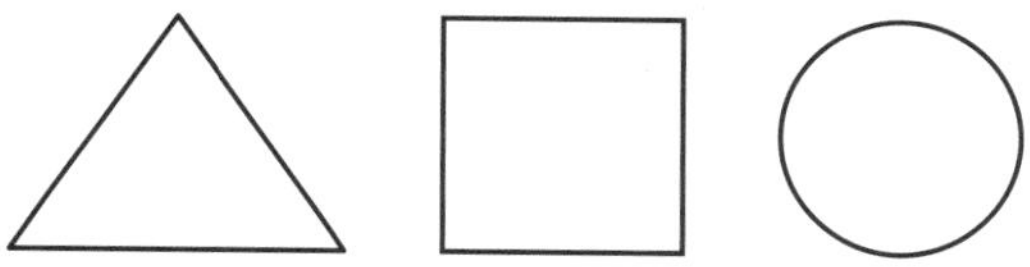

Ⓓ 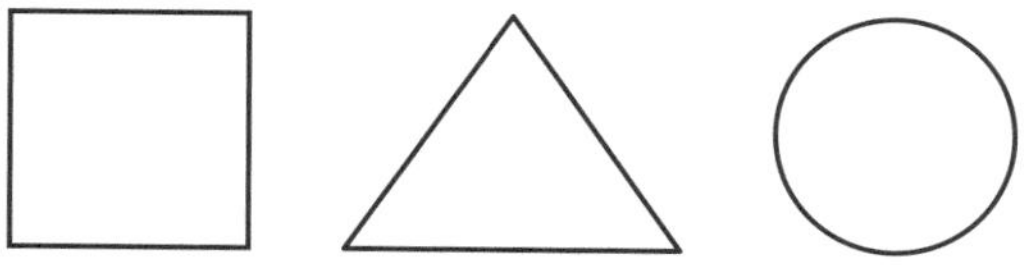

5. Jolene is standing in a row with some children.
She is the 4th from the right and 2nd from the left.
How many children are in the row?

Ⓐ 6 Ⓑ 5 Ⓒ 4 Ⓓ 3

Name: ______________________ Date: ______________

Short Answer

(5 x 2 points = 10 points)

Follow the directions.

6. Color the fifth giraffe from the right.

7. Circle the 4th box from the left.

8. Draw an apple on the 2nd plate.

1st

Name: ______________________ Date: ______________

9. Circle the cat that is under the bench.

10. Look at the picture.
Answer the question.

Who is in front of Carlo? ______________

Name: ______________________ Date: ______________

Extended Response (5 x 1 point = 5 points)

Look at the cards.
Count the dots.
Then fill in the blanks.

11. The 3rd card has ______ dots.

12. The ______ card has only one dot.

13. The ______ card has the most dots.

14. The ______ card has six dots.

15. The ______ card has 1 dot more than the 1st card.

Name: ____________________ Date: ____________

PRE-TEST 7

Numbers to 20

Vocabulary

Fill in the blanks.
Use the words in the box.

make
less than
greater than

1. 1 is ______________ 0.

2. 9 is ______________ 10.

3. 5 and 2 ______________ 7.

Match the number words to the pictures.

4. three • • ☆☆☆☆☆☆☆☆☆

5. eight • • △△△

6. two • • ○○○○○○○○

7. nine • • ◇◇◇◇◇◇

8. six • • □□

Name: ______________________ Date: ______________

Concepts and Skills

Fill in the blanks.

9. 2 more than 8 is ______.

10. ______ is 3 more than 3.

11. ______ is 4 less than 6.

Complete the number patterns.

12.

13.

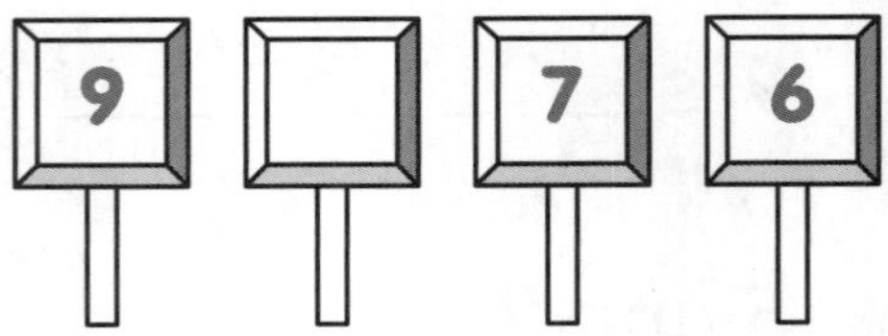

Problem Solving

Circle the set that has fewer.
Then fill in the missing numbers.

14. ______ is less than ______.

15. ______ is more than ______.

Name: ____________________ Date: ____________

TEST PREP 7 Numbers to 20

25

Suggested Time: 30 min

Multiple Choice

(5 x 2 points = 10 points)

Fill in the circle next to the correct answer.

1. Which of these numbers is the least?

Ⓐ twelve Ⓑ twenty Ⓒ eleven Ⓓ sixteen

2. Which number comes just before 13?

Ⓐ 11 Ⓑ 12 Ⓒ 14 Ⓓ 15

3. What number and 6 make 16?

Ⓐ 10 Ⓑ 11 Ⓒ 12 Ⓓ 13

4. What is 2 more than fifteen?

Ⓐ 13 Ⓑ 14 Ⓒ 16 Ⓓ 17

Name: ____________________ Date: ____________

5.

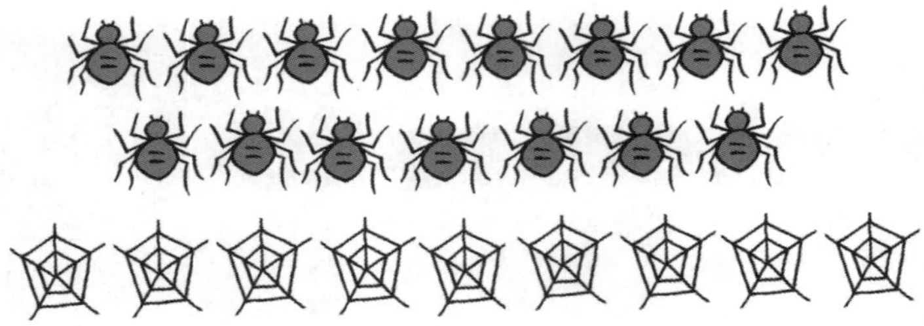

How many fewer 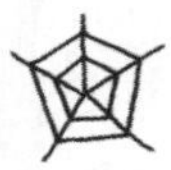 than  are there?

Ⓐ 3 Ⓑ 4 Ⓒ 5 Ⓓ 6

Short Answer

(5 x 2 points = 10 points)

Follow the directions.

6. Write the number.

nineteen	

7. Fill in the blank.

19 = 1 ten ______ ones

8. Fill in the blank.

4 less than 18 is ______.

9. Complete the number pattern.

The missing number is ______.

Name: ______________________________ Date: ______________

10. Order the numbers from greatest to least.

greatest

Extended Response

(5 x 1 point = 5 points)

Count the number of apples each child has. Then fill in the blanks.

11. ______________ has the greatest number of apples.

12. ______________ has the least number of apples.

13. ______________ has 2 more apples than Ryan.

14. Ella has ________ fewer apples than Brad.

15. Brad has ________ more apples than Gina.

Name: ______________________ Date: ____________

PRE-TEST 8

Addition and Subtraction Facts to 20

Vocabulary

Fill in the blanks.
Use the words in the box.

less than	more than	make	subtract	add

1. 8 and 2 ____________ 10.

2. 3 + 7 is the same as 7 ____________ 3.

3. When you ____________ 3 and 5, you get 8.

4. 9 – 1 is the same as 1 ____________ 9.

5. To **take away** is to ____________.

Concepts and Skills

Fill in the blanks.

6. 5 more than 4 is ______.

Name: ______________________ Date: ____________

7. ______ is 5 less than 9.

8. 1 + 6 = ______

9. ______ + 3 = 9

Problem Solving

Solve.
Show your work.

10. Sally has 2 apples.
Lucy has 3 more apples than Sally.
How many apples does Lucy have?

☐ ○ ☐ = ☐

Lucy has ______ apples.

11. There are 9 children in the classroom.
4 children walk out of the classroom.
How many children are left?

☐ ○ ☐ = ☐

There are ______ children left.

Name: ______________________ Date: ______________

TEST PREP 8 Addition and Subtraction Facts to 20

25

Suggested Time: 30 min

Multiple Choice

(5 x 2 points = 10 points)

Fill in the circle next to the correct answer.

1. What is 6 + 13?

Ⓐ 9 Ⓑ 10 Ⓒ 13 Ⓓ 19

2. 14 – ☐ = 5

What is the missing number?

Ⓐ 8 Ⓑ 9 Ⓒ 10 Ⓓ 11

3. The box contains 11 clocks.

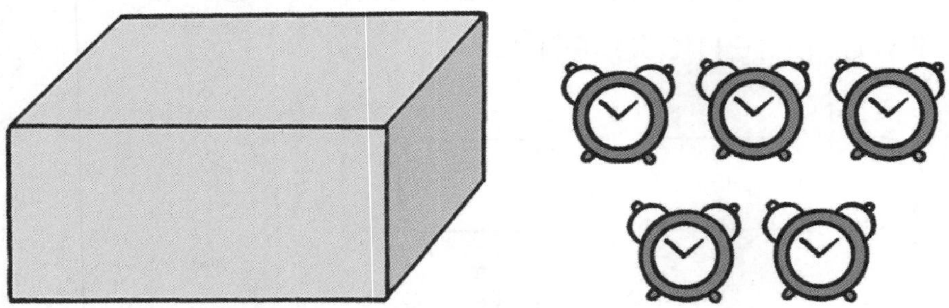

How many clocks are there in all?

Ⓐ 5 Ⓑ 6 Ⓒ 16 Ⓓ 20

Name: ______________________ Date: ____________

4. Sam has 15 marbles.
Some of his marbles are missing.
The rest are in the bottle.
How many marbles are missing?

Ⓐ 18 Ⓑ 12 Ⓒ 9 Ⓓ 3

5.

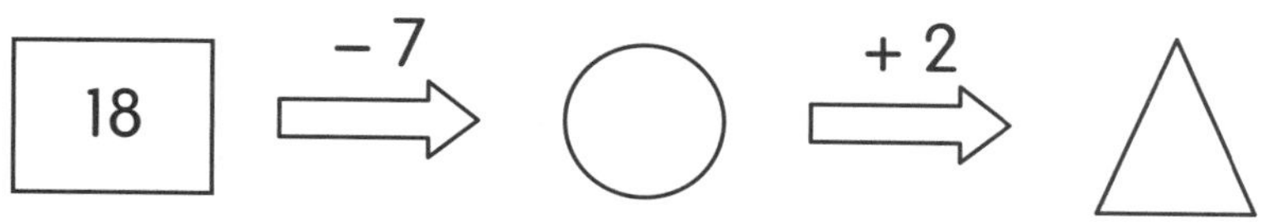

What does  stand for?

Ⓐ 11 Ⓑ 13 Ⓒ 14 Ⓓ 20

Short Answer

(5 x 2 points = 10 points)

Follow the directions.

6. Complete the addition sentence.

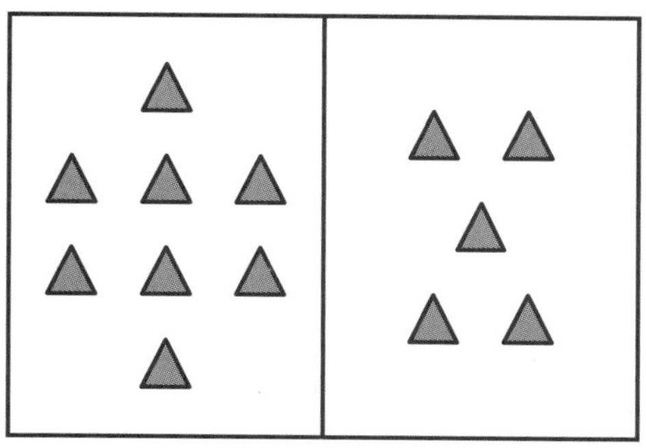

8 + ______ = ______

Name: ______________________ Date: ____________

7. Fill in the blank.

_______ + 8 = 15

8. Complete the subtraction sentence.

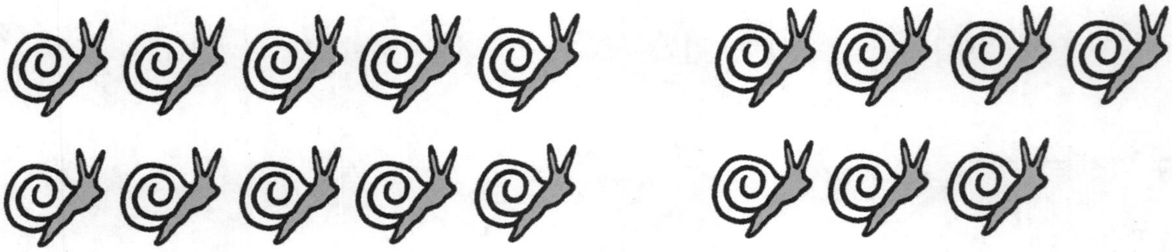

_______ − 9 = _______

9. Fill in the blank.

19 − 8 = 12 − _______

10. Write + or − in the circles.

13 ◯ 3 = 9 ◯ 1

Name: ______________________ Date: ______________

Extended Response

(Question 11: 2 points, Question 12: 3 points)

Solve.
Show your work.

11. Alex has 17 stickers.
Bob has 9 fewer stickers than Alex.
How many stickers does Bob have?

☐ ○ ☐ = ☐

Bob has ______ stickers.

12. Tim has 8 balloons.
Amy has 3 more balloons than Tim.
How many balloons do they have in all?

☐ ○ ☐ = ☐

Amy has ______ balloons.

☐ ○ ☐ = ☐

They have ______ balloons in all.

Name: ______________________ Date: ______________

PRE-TEST 9 Length

Vocabulary

Fill in the blanks.
Use *least* or *greatest*.

7 13 19

1. 7 is the ____________ number.

2. 19 is the ____________ number.

Concepts and Skills

Look at the picture.
Count.
How many are there?

3. There are ______ bells.

Name: ______________________ Date: ______________

TEST PREP 9

Length

25

Suggested Time: 30 min

Multiple Choice

(5 x 2 points = 10 points)

Fill in the circle next to the correct answer.

1.

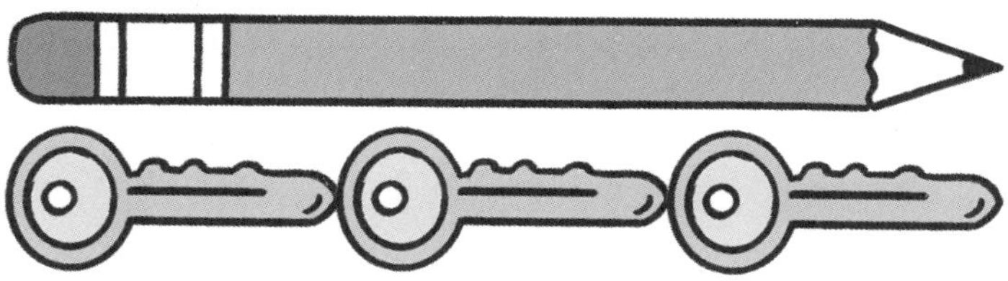

The pencil is about ______  long.

Ⓐ 2 Ⓑ 3 Ⓒ 4 Ⓓ 5

2.

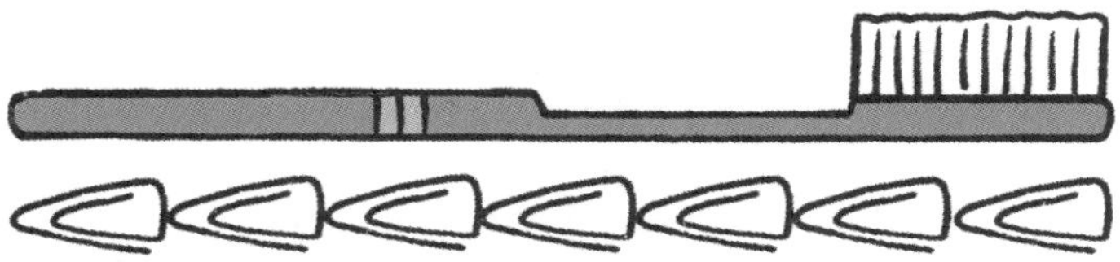

1  stands for 1 unit.

The toothbrush is about ______ units long.

Ⓐ 5 Ⓑ 6 Ⓒ 7 Ⓓ 8

Name: ______________________ Date: ______________

3.

1  stands for 1 unit.

The length of the toy jeep is about _______ units.

Ⓐ 5 Ⓑ 6 Ⓒ 7 Ⓓ 8

Look at the picture.
Answer Exercises 4 and 5.

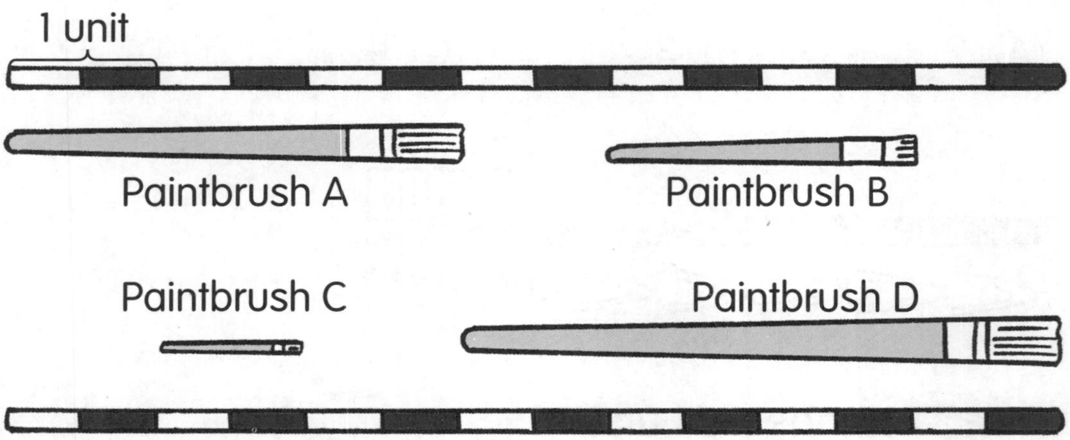

4. Which paintbrush is the longest?

Ⓐ A Ⓑ B Ⓒ C Ⓓ D

5. Which paintbrush is about 2 units long?

Ⓐ A Ⓑ B Ⓒ C Ⓓ D

Name: ______________________ Date: ______________

Short Answer

(5 x 2 points = 10 points)

Follow the directions.

6. Look at the picture.
Color the longer thing.

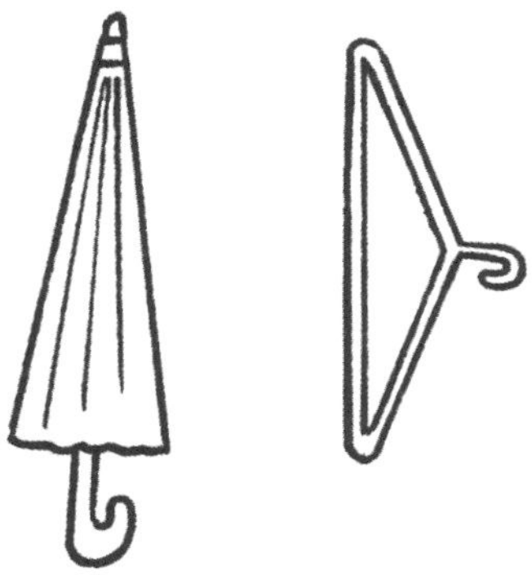

7. Look at the picture.
Circle the shortest tree.

Name: ______________________________ Date: ______________

8.

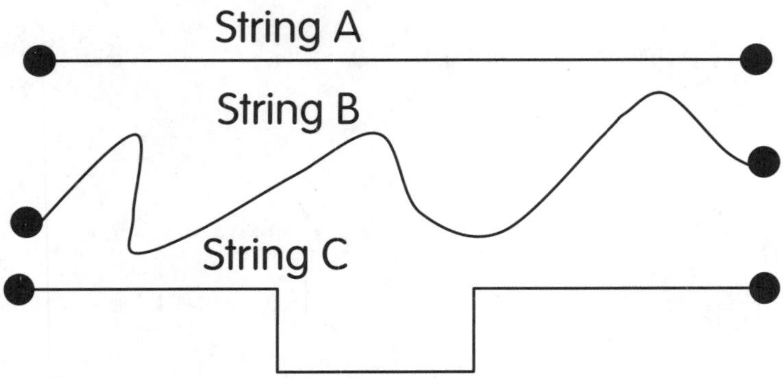

String ______ is the longest.

9.

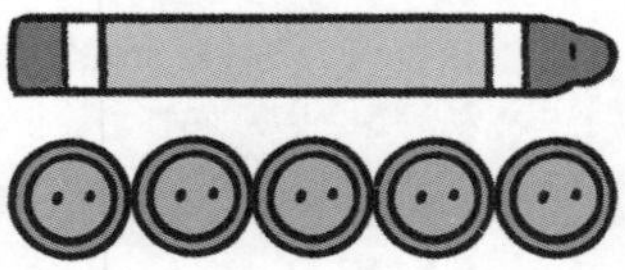

The crayon is about ______  long.

10.

1  stands for 1 unit.

Adam is about ______ units tall.

______ is 10 and ______.

Name: ______________________ Date: ______________

Extended Response
(5 x 1 point = 5 points)

Look at the picture.
The shaded parts show Tapes A, B, C, and D.

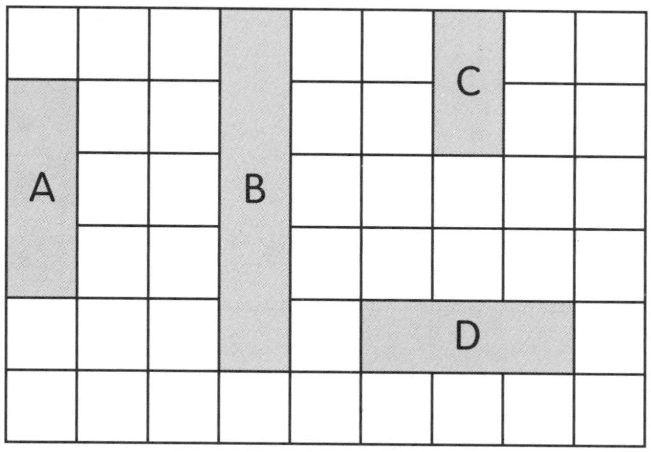

Each □ stands for 1 unit.

11. Tape A is ______ units long.

12. Tape A is as long as Tape ______.

13. Tape D is longer than Tape ______.

14. Tape ______ is the longest.

15. Tape ______ is the shortest.

Name: ____________________ Date: ____________

Mid-Year Test

/100
Suggested Time: 1½ hour

Multiple Choice

(20 x 2 points = 40 points)

Fill in the circle next to the correct answer.

1.

Agnes Bill Calvin Dolly

Which 2 children have the same number of apples?

Ⓐ Agnes and Bill Ⓑ Bill and Calvin

Ⓒ Bill and Dolly Ⓓ Agnes and Dolly

2. Which number bond is correct?

Ⓐ

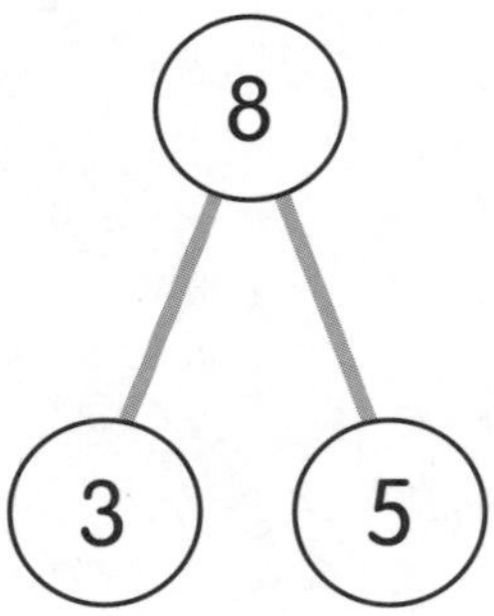

Ⓑ

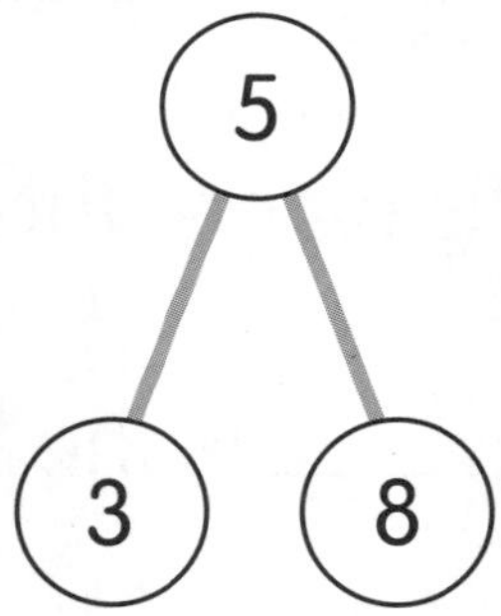

Ⓒ

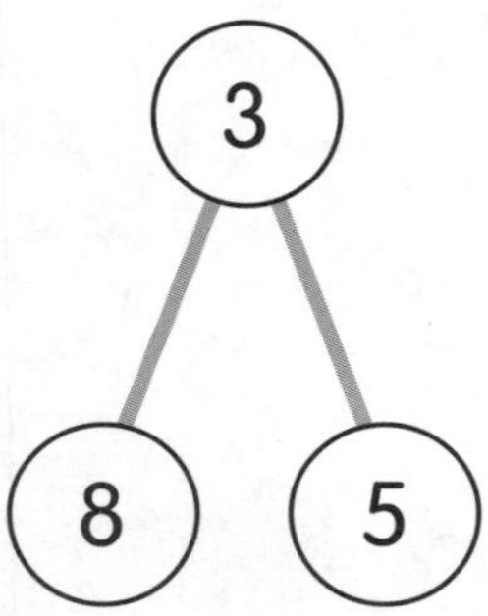

Ⓓ

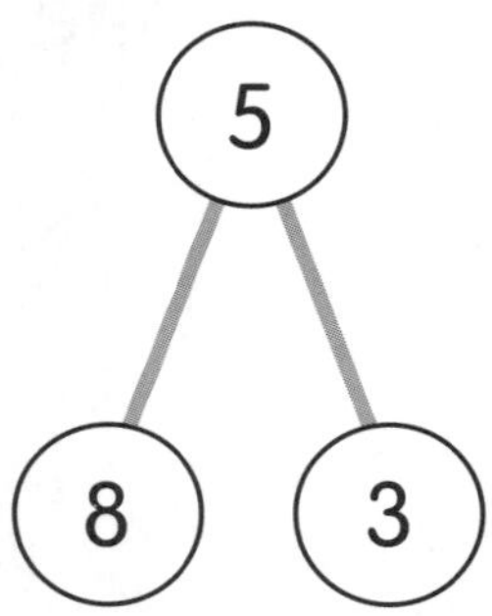

Name: ______________________ Date: ______________

3. Which number is less than 3?

Ⓐ 1 Ⓑ 3 Ⓒ 5 Ⓓ 7

4. What is 4 + 4?

Ⓐ 0 Ⓑ 1 Ⓒ 4 Ⓓ 8

5. 8 + 0 = △ + 6

What is △?

Ⓐ 2 Ⓑ 4 Ⓒ 6 Ⓓ 8

6. What is 2 more than 2 + 3?

Ⓐ 5 Ⓑ 6 Ⓒ 7 Ⓓ 8

7. 9 – ◇ = nine

What is ◇?

Ⓐ 0 Ⓑ 1 Ⓒ 2 Ⓓ 3

8. ♡ – 3 = 2 + 5

What is ♡?

Ⓐ 10 Ⓑ 7 Ⓒ 5 Ⓓ 4

Name: ______________________________ Date: ______________

9. How many triangles are shown in the picture?

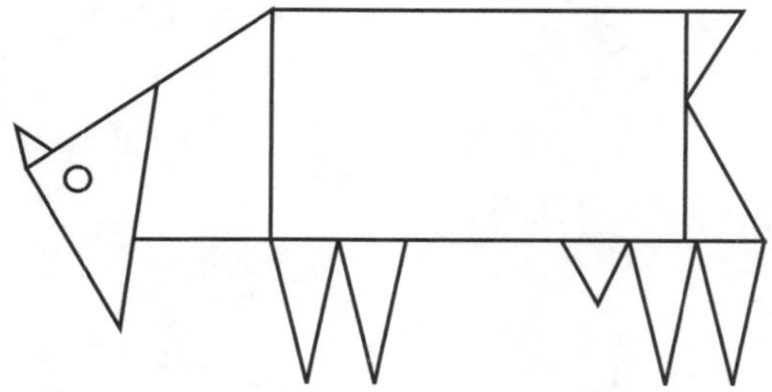

Ⓐ 10 Ⓑ 9 Ⓒ 6 Ⓓ 4

10. Which comes next?

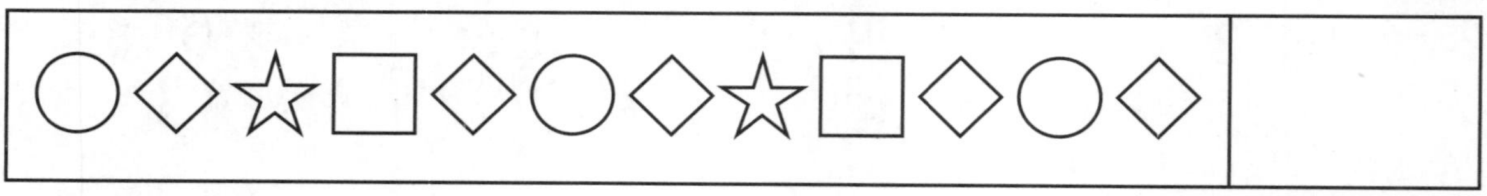

Ⓐ 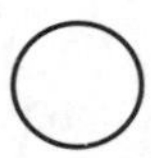 Ⓑ  Ⓒ  Ⓓ 

11.

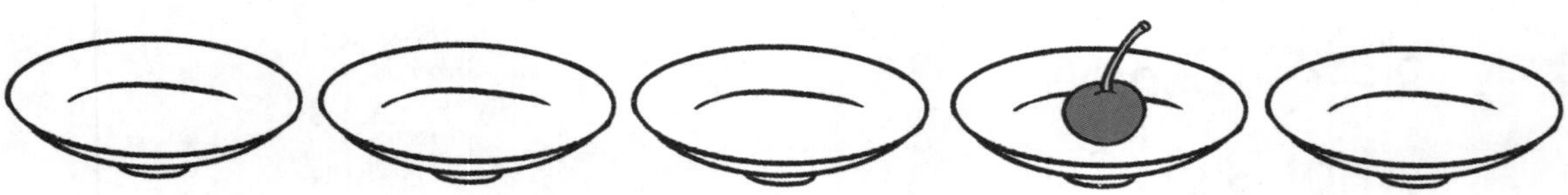

The ______ plate from the left has a cherry on it.

Ⓐ 1st Ⓑ 2nd Ⓒ 3rd Ⓓ 4th

12. 17 is between 16 and .
What is ?

Ⓐ 13 Ⓑ 14 Ⓒ 15 Ⓓ 18

Name: ______________________ Date: ______________

13. Which number is the least?

Ⓐ 18 Ⓑ 13 Ⓒ 20 Ⓓ 15

14. What is 3 more than 12?

Ⓐ 9 Ⓑ 13 Ⓒ 14 Ⓓ 15

15. 16 + 3 = ◯ + 10

What is ◯?

Ⓐ 9 Ⓑ 10 Ⓒ 13 Ⓓ 19

16. What is the same as 2 more than 17?

Ⓐ 8 + 9 Ⓑ 9 + 8 Ⓒ 11 + 7 Ⓓ 10 + 9

17. 20 –  = 15

What is ?

Ⓐ 15 Ⓑ 14 Ⓒ 5 Ⓓ 4

18. Susan has 3 apples.
She also has some oranges.
She has 15 fruits in all.
How many oranges does Susan have?

Ⓐ 2 Ⓑ 8 Ⓒ 12 Ⓓ 18

Name: ____________________ Date: ____________

Look at the pictures.
Answer Exercises 19 and 20.

Each ➡ stands for 1 unit.

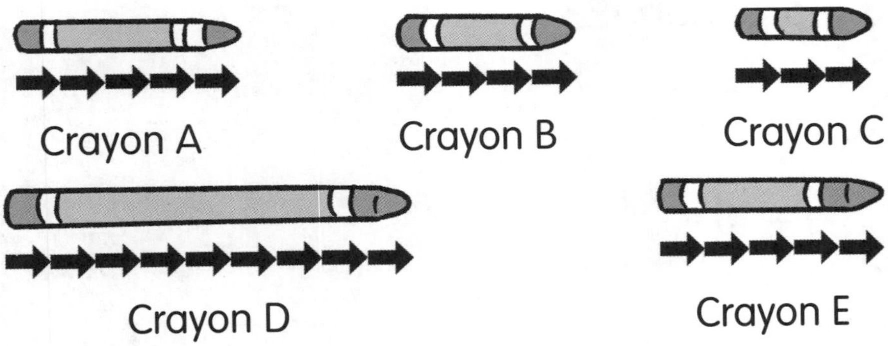

19. Which crayon is as long as Crayon E?

Ⓐ A   Ⓑ B   Ⓒ C   Ⓓ D

20. Which crayon is shorter than Crayon B?

Ⓐ A   Ⓑ C   Ⓒ D   Ⓓ E

Short Answer

(20 x 2 points = 40 points)

Follow the directions.

21. Count the number of leaves.
Then color the same number of flowers.

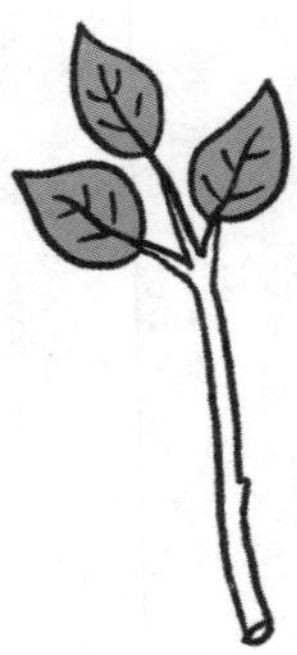

Name: ______________________ Date: ____________

22. Fill in the missing number.

_______ comes just after 8.

23. Look at the number bond.

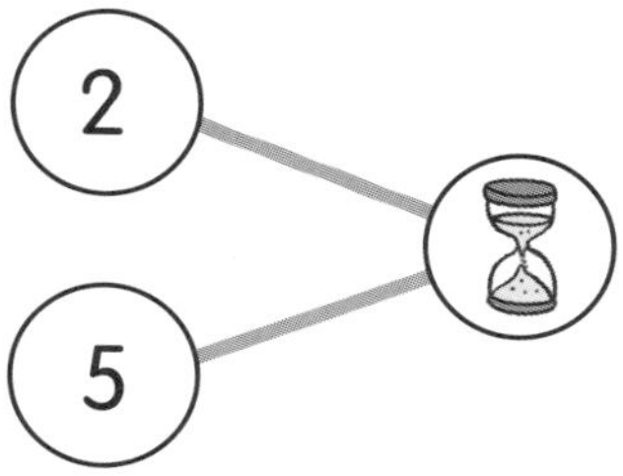

The  stands for _______.

24. Color the two numbers that make 10.

2 3 4 7 9

25. Jimmy has 3 more apples than mushrooms.

?

mushrooms apples

Jimmy has _______ apples.

Name: ______________________ Date: ______________

26. Look at the pictures.
Write the numbers in the boxes.

☐ + ☐ = ☐

27. Color the mug that gives the number in the box.

28. Write a number sentence using the following.

| 8 | 2 | 6 | – | = |

____

29. What comes next?
Color the correct shape.

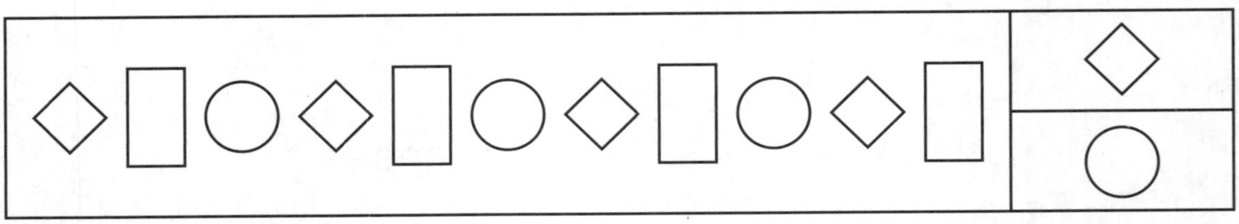

Name: ______________________ Date: ______________

30. Look at the pattern.
What comes next?
Draw the missing dots.

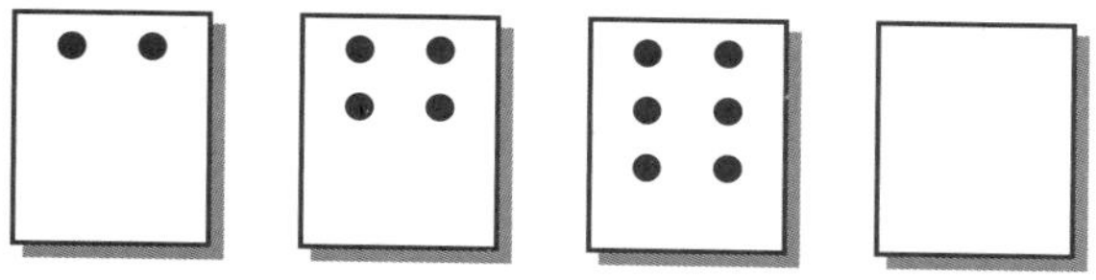

31. The 3rd butterfly has lost a wing.
Circle the 5th butterfly.

32. Draw a flag  on the last boat from the right.

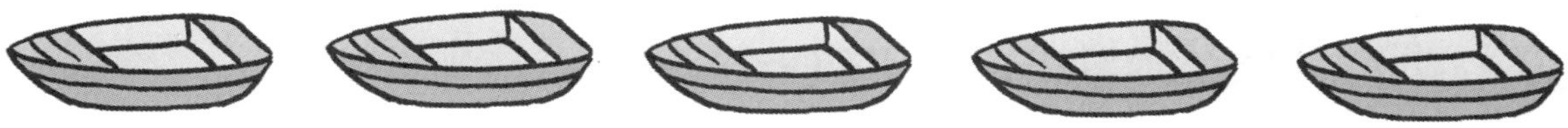

33. Count.
Then write the number in words.

There are ______________ .

Name: ______________________ Date: ______________

34. 5 less than 16 is ______.

35. Arrange the numbers in order, beginning with the least.

14 19 11 13

least

36. Fill in the blank.

11 + ______ = 20

37. Fill in the missing number.

12 + 5 = ______ + 9

38. Fill in the blank.

20 – 7 = ______ – 1

Name: ______________________ Date: ____________

39. Look at the picture.
Each  stands for 1 unit.

The length of the watch is about ______ units.

40. Look at the picture.
How tall is the door?

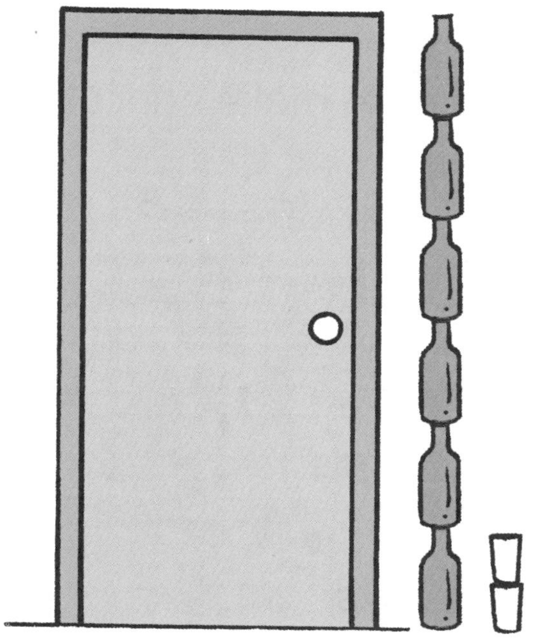

The door is about ______  tall.

Name: ______________________ Date: ______________

Extended Response

(5 x 4 points = 20 points)

Solve.
Show your work.

41. Jessie has 5 red ribbons.
She also has 3 yellow ribbons.
How many ribbons does Jessie have in all?

☐ ◯ ☐ = ☐

Jessie has ______ ribbons in all.

42. Mike buys 10 eggs.
He uses some eggs to make pancakes.
He has 8 eggs left.
How many eggs does Mike use?

☐ ◯ ☐ = ☐

Mike uses ______ eggs.

43. Amy has 11 storybooks.
Her brother gives her 3 more storybooks.
How many storybooks does Amy have in all?

☐ ◯ ☐ = ☐

Amy has ______ storybooks in all.

Name: ______________________________ Date: ______________

44. Carlos and John have 19 marbles in all.
Carlos has 11 marbles.
How many marbles does John have?

[ ] ( ) [ ] = [ ]

John has ______ marbles.

45. Pauline has 12 markers.
She gives 5 markers to her brother.
How many markers does Pauline have left?

[ ] ( ) [ ] = [ ]

Pauline has ______ markers left.

Name: ____________________ Date: ____________

Bonus Questions

Follow the directions.

1. Complete the Magic Square.
Use all the numbers from 1 to 9.
The numbers in a row (←→), column (↕) or diagonal (↗, ↘), must add up to 15.
Some squares have been filled for you.

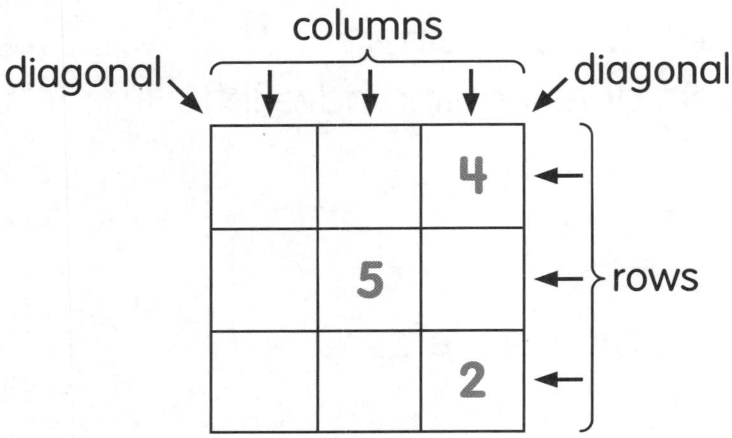

2. Write the missing numbers in the shapes.

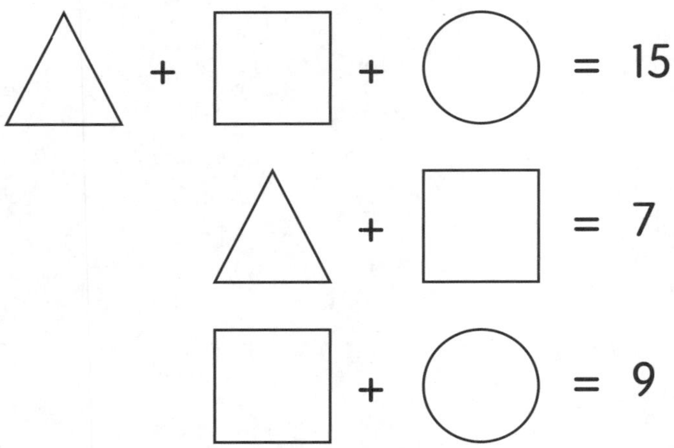

Name: ______________________ Date: ______________

PRE-TEST 10 Weight

Vocabulary

Fill in the blanks.
Use *heavier* or *lighter*.

1.

The pencil is ______________ than the book.

2.

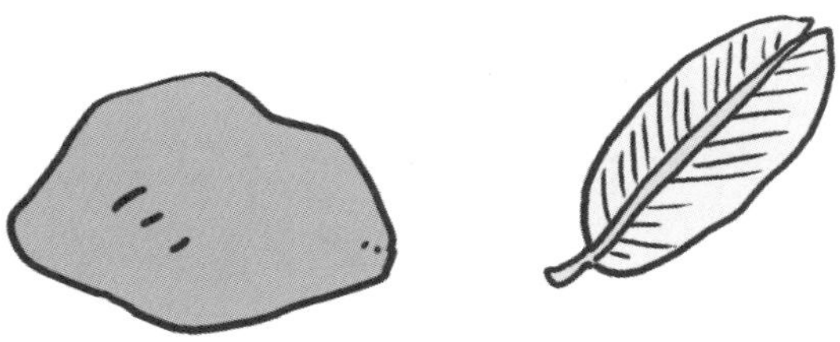

The rock is ______________ than the feather.

Name: ______________________ Date: ______________

Concepts and Skills

Circle the heavier object.

3.

4.

Circle the lighter object.

5.

6.

Name: ______________________ Date: ______________

Problem Solving

Compare.
Look at the pictures.
Then fill in the blanks.

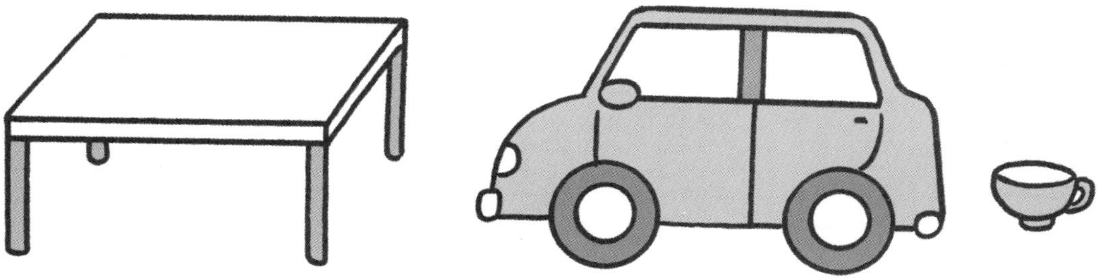

7. The ____________ is lighter than the table.

8. The ____________ is the lightest.

9. The ____________ is the heaviest.

10. Order the things from lightest to heaviest.

____________, ____________, ____________
lightest

Name: ______________________ Date: ______________

TEST PREP 10 Weight

25

Suggested Time: 30 min

Multiple Choice

(5 x 2 points = 10 points)

Fill in the circle next to the correct answer.

1.

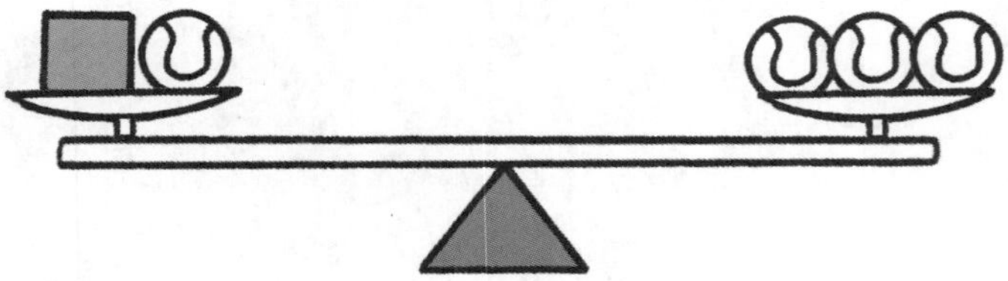

The weight of the box is about ______ .

Ⓐ 1 Ⓑ 2 Ⓒ 3 Ⓓ 4

2.

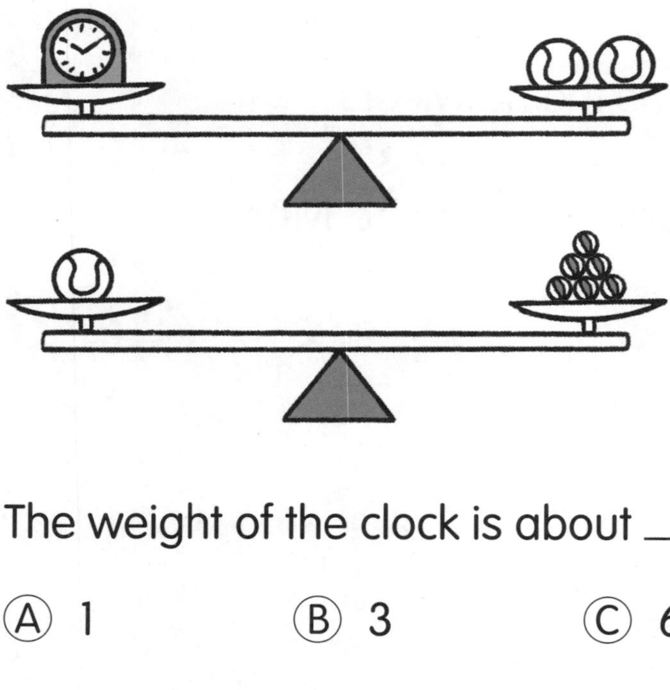

The weight of the clock is about ______ marbles.

Ⓐ 1 Ⓑ 3 Ⓒ 6 Ⓓ 12

Name: ______________________ Date: ______________

Look at the picture.
Answer Exercises 3 and 4.

Use ● as 1 unit.

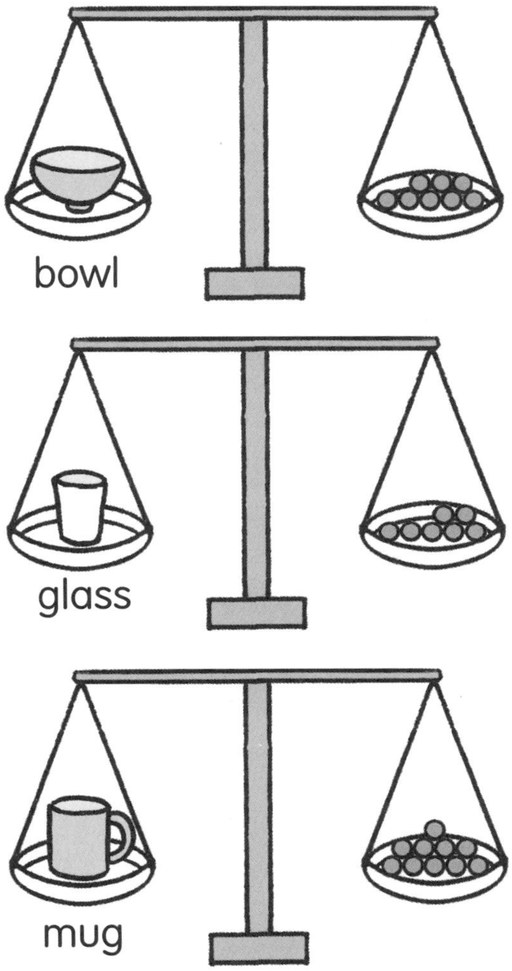

3. The weight of the mug is ______ units.

Ⓐ 7 Ⓑ 8 Ⓒ 9 Ⓓ 10

4. The ______ is heavier than the ______.

Ⓐ bowl, glass Ⓑ bowl, mug

Ⓒ glass, bowl Ⓓ glass, mug

Name: ______________________ Date: ______________

5.

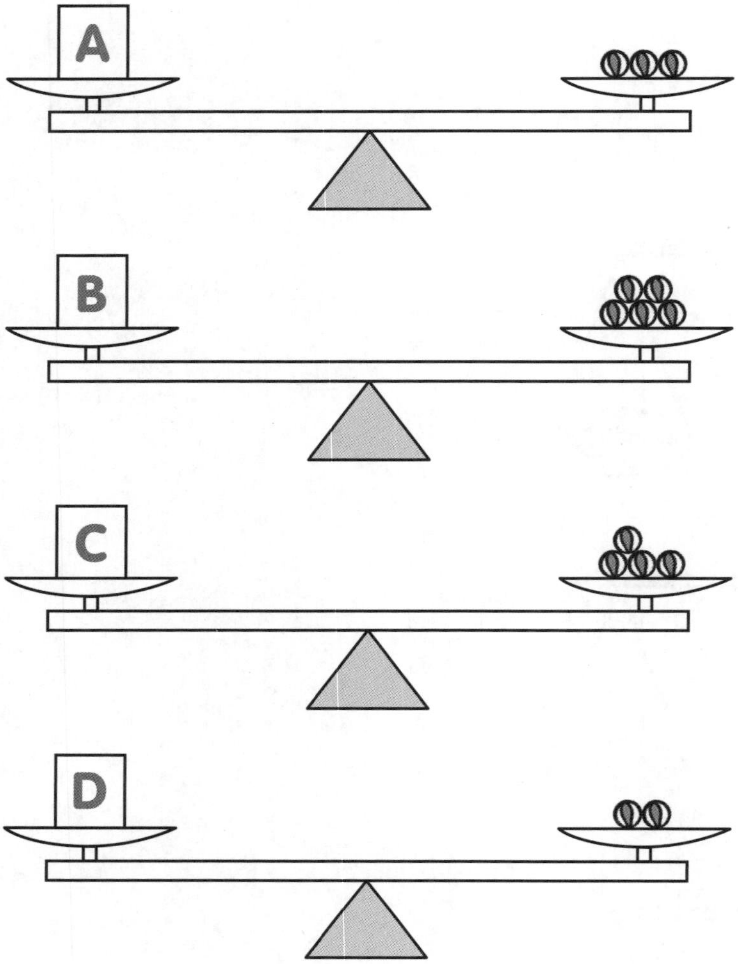

Box ______ is as heavy as 4 .

Ⓐ A   Ⓑ B   Ⓒ C   Ⓓ D

Name: ______________________ Date: ______________

Short Answer

(5 x 2 points = 10 points)

Follow the directions.

6. Circle the heavier animal.

7. Fill in the blank.
Use *heavier* or *lighter.*

The feather is ______________ than the pear.

Name: ______________________ Date: ______________

Look at the pictures.
Fill in the blanks.

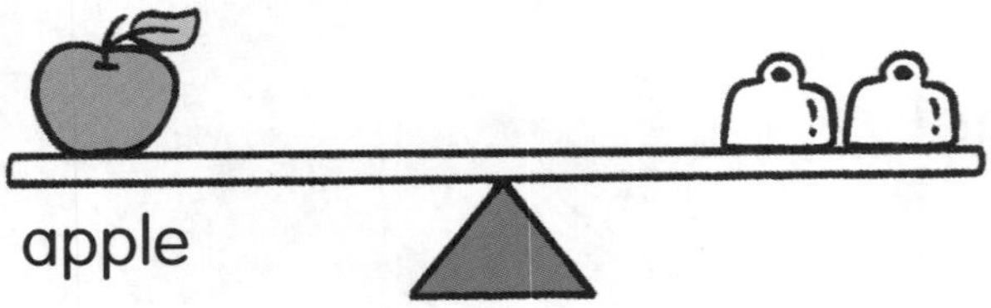

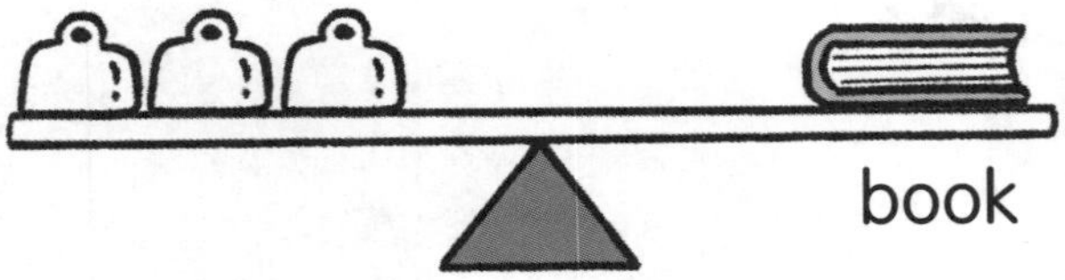

8. The weight of the book is about ______ 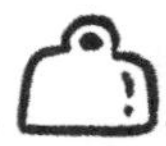.

9. The ______________ is heavier than the ______________.

Look at the pictures.
Fill in the blank.

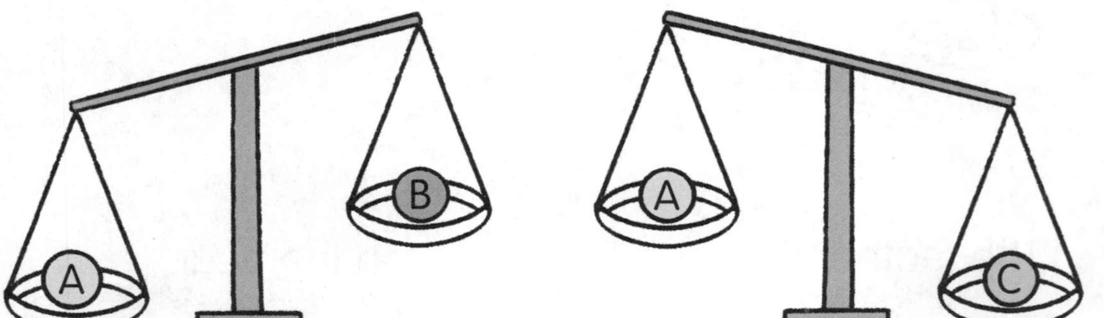

10. Ball ______ is lightest.

Name: ______________________________ Date: ______________

Extended Response

(Questions 11 to 13: 3 x 1 point = 3 points,
Question 14: 2 points)

**Look at the pictures.
Then fill in the blanks.**

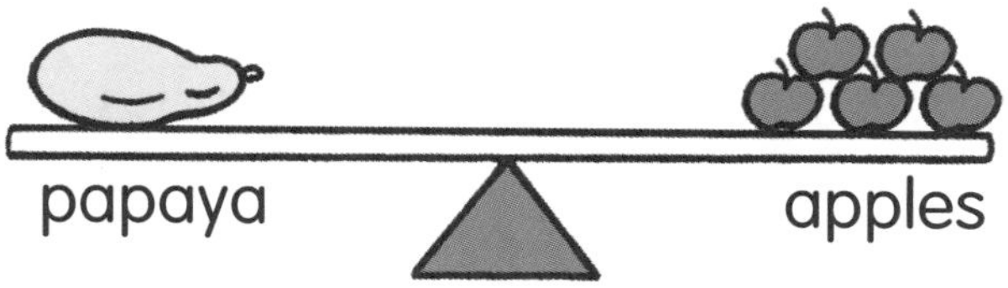

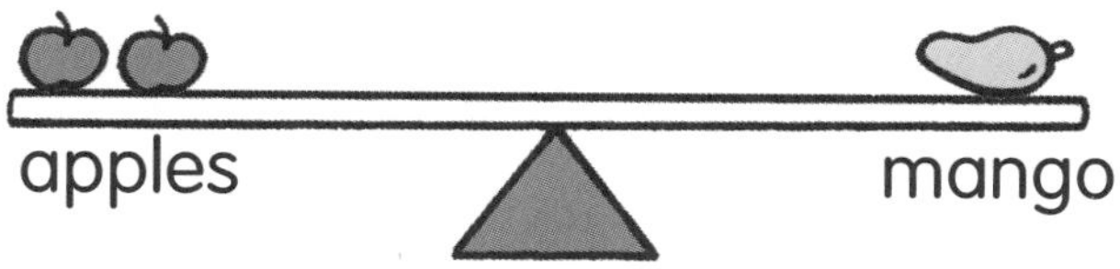

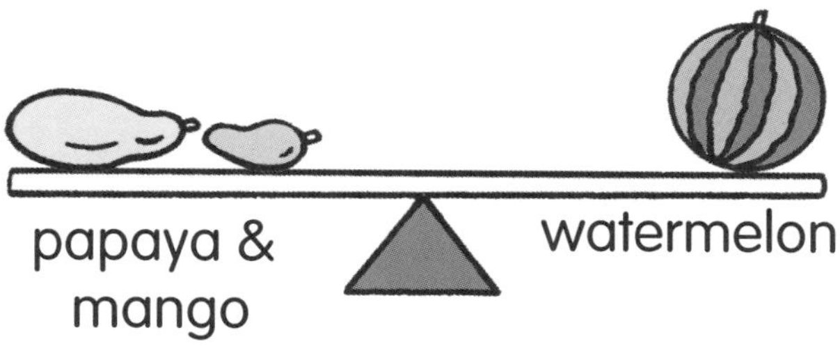

11. The weight of the mango is about ________ apples.

12. The weight of the papaya is about ________ apples.

13. The heaviest fruit is the ______________.

14. Order the fruits from heaviest to lightest.

heaviest

Name: ______________________ Date: ______________

PRE-TEST 11

Picture Graphs and Bar Graphs

Vocabulary

Fill in the blanks.
Use the words in the box.

more	same	fewer

1.

There are ______________ flowers than bees.

2.

There are ______________ cups than glasses.

Name: ______________________ Date: ______________

3. 

There are the ______ number of cats and rabbits.

Concepts and Skills

Fill in the blanks.

4. 2 more than 4 is ______.

5. ______ is 3 more than 5.

6. 4 less than 5 is ______.

7. ______ is 1 less than 8.

Name: ____________________ Date: ____________

Problem Solving

Count and compare.
Fill in the blanks.

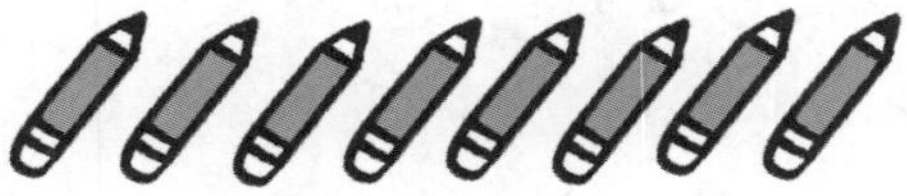

pencils

paper clips

erasers

rulers

8. There are ______ more pencils than erasers.

9. There is/are ______ fewer paper clip(s) than rulers.

10. There are the same number of __________ and

__________.

Name: ______________________ Date: ______________

Test Prep 11 Picture Graphs and Bar Graphs

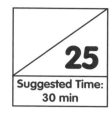

25

Suggested Time: 30 min

Multiple Choice (5 x 2 points = 10 points)

Fill in the circle next to the correct answer.

Look at the picture graph.

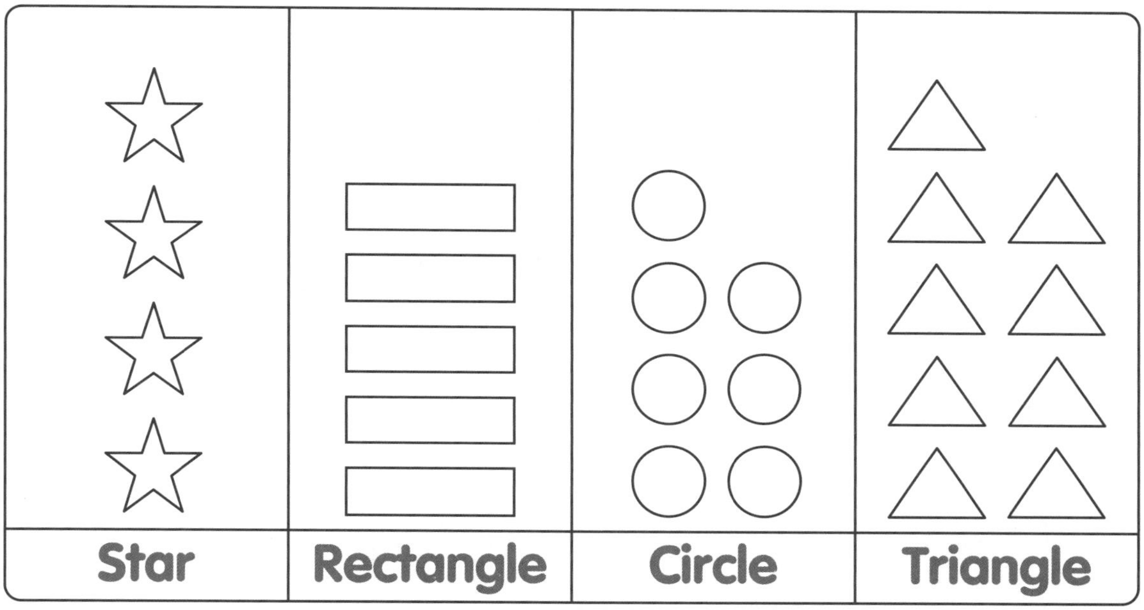

1. How many more triangles than rectangles are there?

Ⓐ 4 Ⓑ 5 Ⓒ 9 Ⓓ 14

2. How many stars and circles are there in all?

Ⓐ 3 Ⓑ 4 Ⓒ 7 Ⓓ 11

Name: ______________________________ Date: ______________

Look at the bar graph.

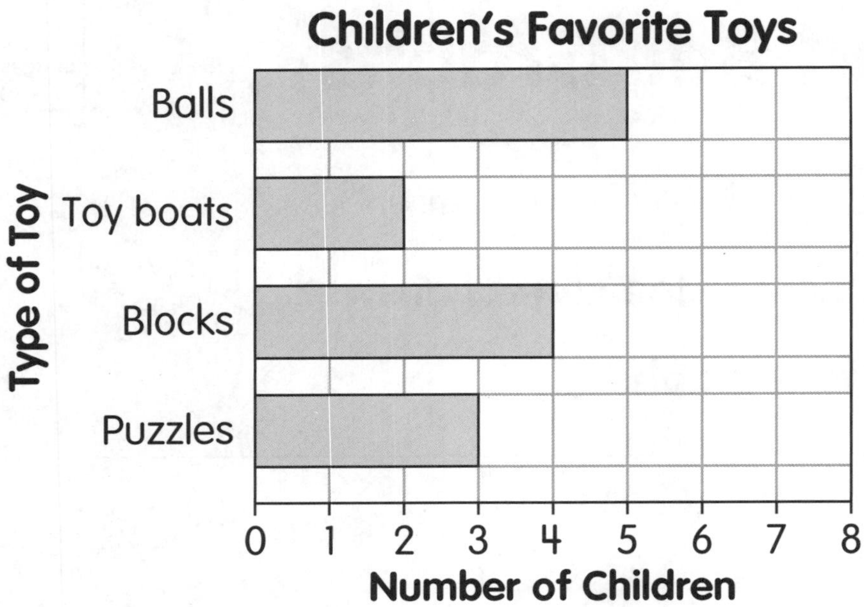

3. Which tally marks show the number of children who like blocks or puzzles?

Ⓐ |||| Ⓑ 𝍸 Ⓒ 𝍸 | Ⓓ 𝍸 ||

4. How many fewer children like toy boats than blocks?

Ⓐ 1 Ⓑ 2 Ⓒ 4 Ⓓ 6

5. Which is the favorite toy for the greatest number of children?

Ⓐ balls Ⓑ toy boats

Ⓒ blocks Ⓓ puzzles

Name: ______________________ Date: ______________

Short Answer (5 x 2 points = 10 points)

Follow the directions.

Look at the picture graph.
Fill in the blanks.

Our Marble Collections

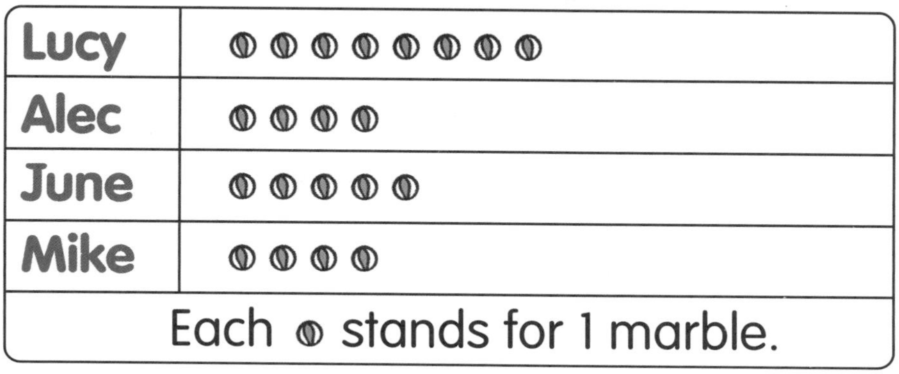

Lucy
Alec
June
Mike
Each stands for 1 marble.

6. Alec and ______________ have the same number of marbles.

7. Lucy and June have ________ marbles in all.

8. Mike has ________ fewer marbles than Lucy.

Name: ______________________ Date: ______________

Look at the bar graph.
Fill in the blanks.

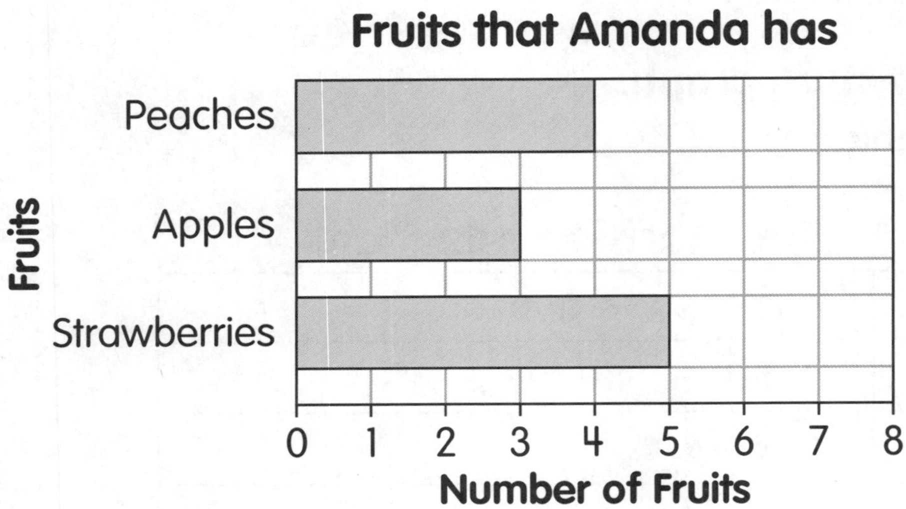

9. There are ______ more strawberries than apples.

10. There are ______ fruits in all.

Name: ______________________ Date: ______________

Extended Response

(5 x 1 point = 5 points)

Look at the picture graph.
Fill in the blanks.

Birthday Month of Children in the Class

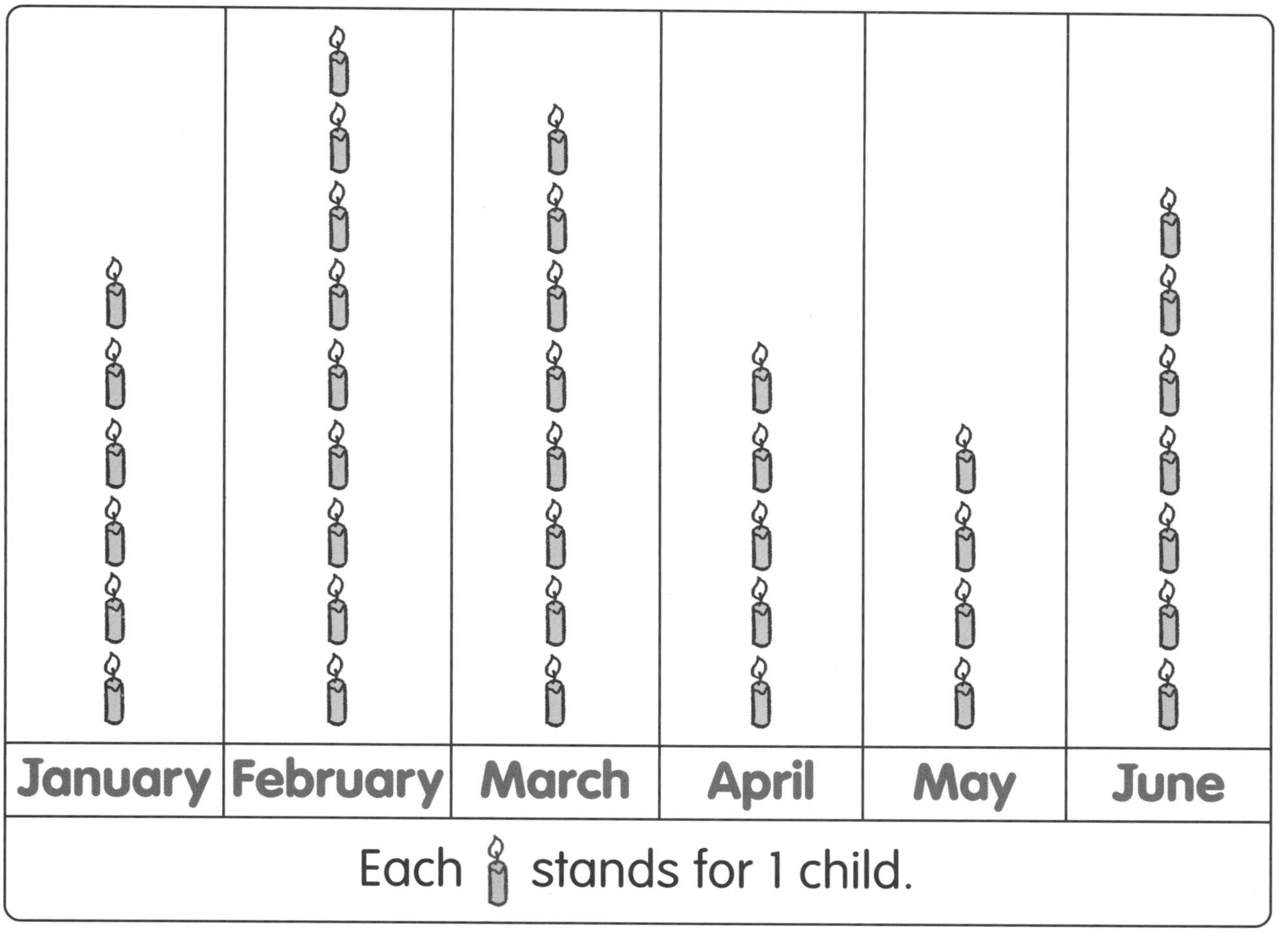

11. ______ children were born in May.

12. ______ more children were born in March than in April.

13. The most number of birthdays are in __________.

14. There are ______ children born in January and February.

15. There are 2 fewer birthdays in __________ than in June.

Name: ______________________ Date: ______________

PRE-TEST 12

Numbers to 40

Vocabulary

Fill in the blanks.
Use the words in the box.

make
less than
greater than

1. 9 is ______________ 11.

2. 18 is ______________ 13.

3. 15 and 2 ______________ 17.

Count and write the numbers in the boxes.
Then write the numbers in words.

4.	☆☆☆☆☆ ☆☆☆☆ ☆☆☆☆☆	☐ ______________
5.	△△△△△ △ △△△△△	☐ ______________
6.	○○○○○ ○○○ ○○○○○	☐ ______________
7.	◇◇◇◇◇ ◇◇◇◇◇ ◇◇◇◇◇ ◇	☐ ______________
8.	□□□□□ □□□□ □□□□□ □□□□	☐ ______________

Name: ____________________ Date: __________

Concepts and Skills

Fill in the blanks.

9. 2 more than 16 is ______.

10. 5 less than 15 is ______.

11. ______ is 3 more than 13.

12. ______ is 4 less than 17.

Complete the number patterns.

13. 11, 13, ______, 17, ______

14. 20, ______, 16, ______, 12, 10, 8

Problem Solving

Compare.
Fill in the missing numbers.

15 19 11

15. ______ is less than 15.

16. ______ is greater than 15.

17. ______ is the greatest.

18. Order the numbers from least to greatest.

______, ______, ______
least

Name: ______________________ Date: ______________

TEST PREP

12 Numbers to 40

25
Suggested Time: 30 min

Multiple Choice

(5 x 2 points = 10 points)

Fill in the circle next to the correct answer.

1. What number does the place-value chart show?

Tens	Ones
3	2

Ⓐ five Ⓑ twenty-three

Ⓒ thirty Ⓓ thirty-two

2. Which two numbers have a 3 in the tens place?

Ⓐ 13, 34 Ⓑ 37, 30 Ⓒ 33, 23 Ⓓ 30, 15

3. 30 is ______ tens and 10 ones.

Ⓐ 2 Ⓑ 3 Ⓒ 20 Ⓓ 30

4. 28 is less than ______ but more than ______.

Ⓐ 25, 27 Ⓑ 29, 31 Ⓒ 35, 30 Ⓓ 36, 26

5. What is the missing number in the number pattern?

15, 20, 25, 30, ______

Ⓐ 31 Ⓑ 32 Ⓒ 34 Ⓓ 35

Name: ______________________ Date: ______________

Short Answer

(5 x 2 points = 10 points)

Follow the directions.

6. Count.
Then write the number.

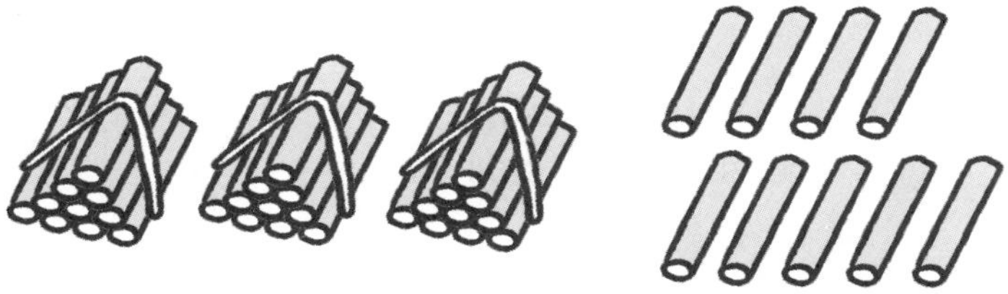

7. Write the number in words.

40	

8. Write the missing numbers.

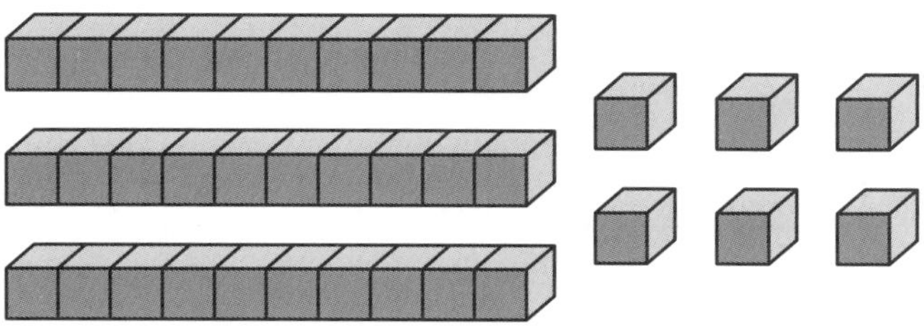

______ tens ______ ones

Name: ______________________ Date: ______________

9. Write the missing number.

_______ is 5 more than 18.

10. Complete the number pattern.

18, _______, 22, _______, 26, 28

Extended Response

(Questions 11 to 13: 3 x 1 point = 3 points, Question 14: 2 points)

Look at the numbers.
Fill in the blanks.

11. _______ is 6 more than 26.

12. _______ is 3 less than 29.

13. The greatest number is _______.

14. Order the numbers from least to greatest.

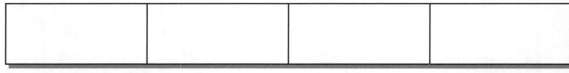

least			

Name: ______________________ Date: ______________

PRE-TEST 13

Addition and Subtraction to 40

Vocabulary

Fill in the blanks.
Use the words in the box.

make	subtract	doubles fact

1. We can use a ____________ to solve the problem:

5 + 6 = ________.

2. 8 and 2 ____________ 10.

3. We can ____________ by grouping into tens and ones.

Concepts and Skills

Add using a doubles fact.

4. 6 + 7 = ________

Name: ______________________ Date: ______________

Add by grouping the numbers into a ten and ones.

5. 12 + 5 = ______

Subtract by grouping the numbers into a ten and ones.

6. 18 − 6 = ______

7. 11 − 4 = ______

Problem Solving

Solve.
Show your work.

8. Amanda paints 9 stars red.
She paints 5 more blue stars than red stars.
How many blue stars does Amanda paint?

☐ ○ ☐ = ☐

Amanda paints ______ blue stars.

9. Thomas catches 12 bugs.
He catches 3 more bugs than Roger.
How many bugs does Roger catch?

☐ ○ ☐ = ☐

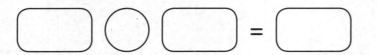

Roger catches ______ bugs.

Name: ______________________ Date: ____________

TEST PREP 13 Addition and Subtraction to 40

	25
Suggested Time: 30 min	

Multiple Choice

(5 x 2 points = 10 points)

Fill in the circle next to the correct answer.

1. 26 + 4 = 10 + ☐

Ⓐ 10 Ⓑ 20 Ⓒ 30 Ⓓ 40

2. What is the same as 3 less than 31?

Ⓐ 20 + 3 Ⓑ 18 + 4 Ⓒ 26 + 8 Ⓓ 22 + 6

3. What is equal to 32?

Ⓐ 20 + 3 Ⓑ 30 – 2 Ⓒ 28 + 2 Ⓓ 40 – 8

4. 29 – ☐ = 12

Ⓐ 12 Ⓑ 15 Ⓒ 17 Ⓓ 39

5. Susan buys 11 buns.
Tom buys 5 fewer buns.
How many buns does Tom buy?

Ⓐ 6 Ⓑ 9 Ⓒ 16 Ⓓ 61

Name: ______________________ Date: ______________

Short Answer (5 x 2 points = 10 points)

Follow the directions.

6. Fill in the missing number.

3 less than 36 is ______.

7. Add.

$$\begin{array}{r} 12 \\ +\ 16 \\ \hline \end{array}$$

8. Subtract.

$$\begin{array}{r} 38 \\ -\ 29 \\ \hline \end{array}$$

9. Fill in the missing number.

23 + ______ = 37

10. Fill in the missing number.

3 + 5 + 7 = ______

Name: ______________________ Date: ______________

Extended Response

(Question 11: 2 points, Question 12: 3 points)

Solve.
Show your work.

11. Tim and Sam caught 37 fish in all.
Sam caught 14 fish.
How many fish did Tim catch?

☐ ○ ☐ = ☐

Tim caught ______ fish.

12. A pet shop has 15 kittens, 10 puppies, and 7 bunnies.
How many pets does the pet shop have in all?

☐ ○ ☐ ○ ☐ = ☐

The pet shop has ______ pets in all.

Name: ______________________ Date: ______________

Pre-Test 14 Mental Math Strategies

Vocabulary

Fill in the blanks.
Use the words in the box.

doubles facts
regroup
make

1. 7 and 3 ______________ 10.

2. 5 + 5 and 8 + 8 are ______________.

3. We can ______________ 12 ones into 1 ten and 2 ones.

Concepts and Skills

Complete the fact family.

4.

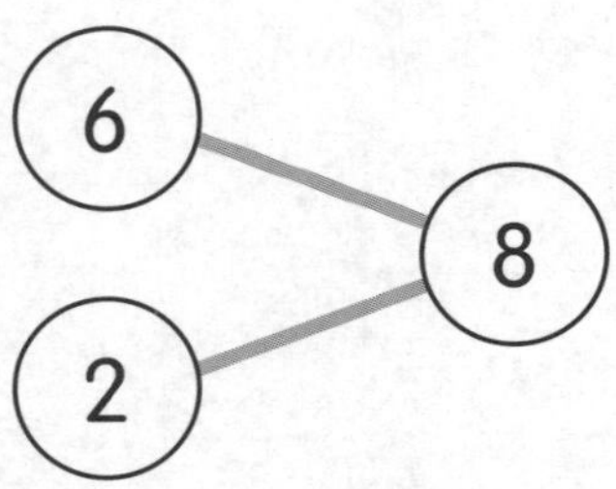

6 + 2 = ☐

☐ + ☐ = ☐

☐ − ☐ = ☐

☐ − ☐ = ☐

Name: ______________________ Date: ______________

Add or subtract.

5. $5 + 9 =$ ______

6. $21 + 5 =$ ______

7. $23 - 6 =$ ______

8. $31 - 5 =$ ______

Problem Solving

Solve.

9. Kelly has 25 story books.
Her friend gives her 6 more story books.
How many story books does Kelly have now?

☐ ◯ ☐ = ☐

Kelly has ______ story books now.

10. Jason sells 17 packets of greeting cards.
He has 12 packets left.
How many packets did he start with?

☐ ◯ ☐ = ☐

Jason started with ______ packets.

Name: ______________________ Date: ______________

Test Prep 14 Mental Math Strategies

25
Suggested Time: 30 min

Multiple Choice

(5 x 2 points = 10 points)

Add or subtract.
Use mental math.
Fill in the circle next to the correct answer.

1. What is 8 + 9?

Ⓐ 5 Ⓑ 7 Ⓒ 15 Ⓓ 17

2. What is 20 + 17?

Ⓐ 3 Ⓑ 27 Ⓒ 30 Ⓓ 37

3. What is 16 – 7?

Ⓐ 1 Ⓑ 9 Ⓒ 10 Ⓓ 11

4. What is 38 – 6?

Ⓐ 22 Ⓑ 30 Ⓒ 32 Ⓓ 36

5. What is 27 – 10?

Ⓐ 7 Ⓑ 12 Ⓒ 13 Ⓓ 17

Name: ______________________ Date: ______________

Short Answer

(5 x 2 points = 10 points)

Add or subtract.
Use mental math.

6. $21 + 8 =$ _______

7. $35 + 3 =$ _______

8. $18 + 20 =$ _______

9. $26 - 4 =$ _______

10. $39 - 20 =$ _______

Extended Response

(Question 11: 2 points, Question 12: 3 points)

Solve.
Use mental math.

11. Lucy has 19 flowers.
Her friend gives her 10 more flowers.
How many flowers does Lucy have in all?

Lucy has _______ flowers in all.

Name: ______________________ Date: ______________

12. A pond has 26 ducks.
Some ducks fly away.
5 ducks are left at the pond.
How many ducks flew away?

_______ ducks flew away.

Name: ____________________ Date: ____________

PRE-TEST 15

Calendar and Time

Vocabulary

Fill in the blanks.
Use the words in the box.

morning	week	night	time

1. There are 7 days in a ____________.

2. We use a clock to tell ____________.

3. We go to school in the ____________.

4. We go to bed at ____________.

Concepts and Skills

Write the time.

5. 

______ o'clock

Name: ______________________ Date: ______________

6.

_______ o'clock

7.

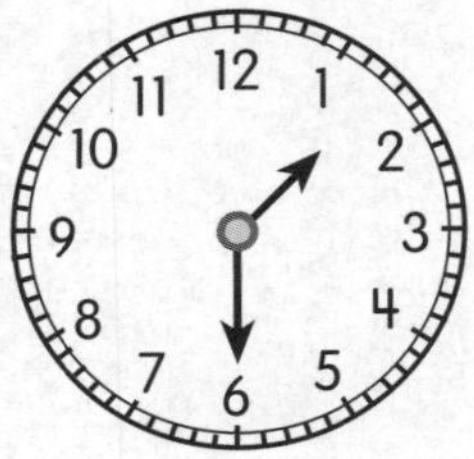

half past _______

8.

half past _______

Name: ______________________________ Date: ______________

Problem Solving

Put the events in order from morning to night.
Write 1, 2, 3, and 4 in the boxes.

9.

Name: ______________________ Date: ____________

TEST PREP

15 Calendar and Time

25
Suggested Time: 30 min

Multiple Choice

(5 x 2 points = 10 points)

Fill in the circle next to the correct answer.

Look at the calendar.
Answer Exercises 1 and 2.

February						
Sunday	**Monday**	**Tuesday**	**Wednesday**	**Thursday**	**Friday**	**Saturday**
1	2	3	4	5	6	7
8	9	10	11	12	13	14
15	16	17	18	19	20	21
22	23	24	25	26	27	28

1. What day is February 20?

Ⓐ Tuesday Ⓑ Wednesday

Ⓒ Thursday Ⓓ Friday

2. On what day of the week will the next month start?

Ⓐ Sunday Ⓑ Monday

Ⓒ Tuesday Ⓓ Friday

Name: ______________________________ Date: ______________

3. Look at the clock.
What time is it?

Ⓐ 2 o'clock Ⓑ half past 2

Ⓒ 3 o'clock Ⓓ half past 3

4.

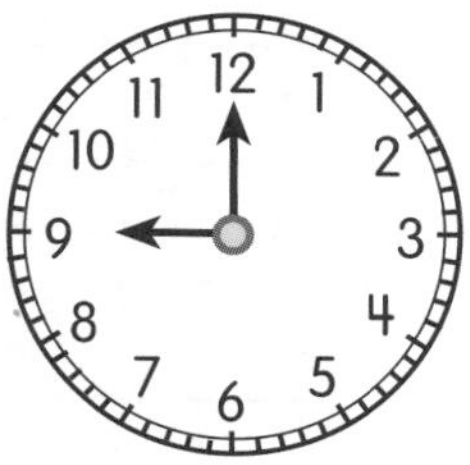

Alison

Ben

Charlie

Danny

Four children go to bed at different times at night.
Who goes to bed last?

Ⓐ Alison Ⓑ Ben Ⓒ Charlie Ⓓ Danny

5. Which clock shows half past 6?

Ⓐ

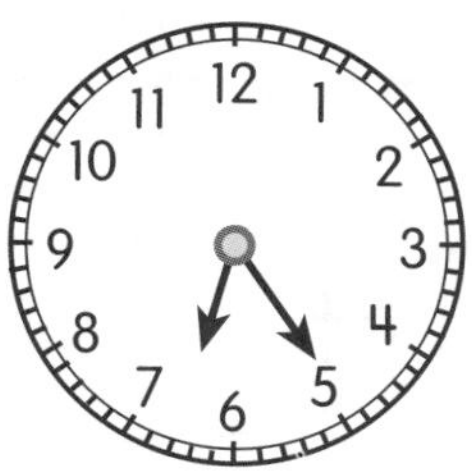

Ⓑ

Ⓒ

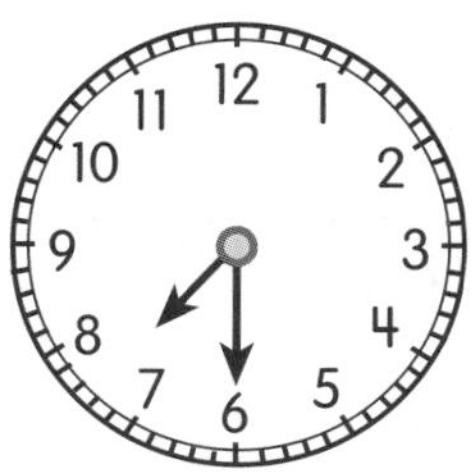

Ⓓ

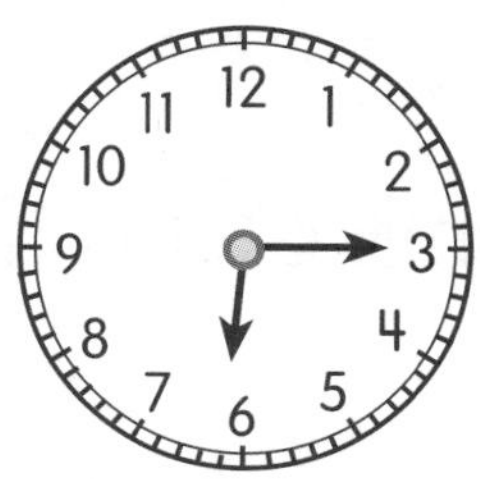

Name: ______________________ Date: ____________

Short Answer (5 x 2 points = 10 points)

Follow the directions.

6. Look at the calendar.

April						
Sunday	Monday	Tuesday	Wednesday	Thursday	Friday	Saturday
				1	2	3
4	5	6	7	8	9	10
11	12	13	14	15	16	17
18	19	20	21	22	23	24
25	26	27	28	29	30	

The date of the last Saturday of April is ________.

7. Look at the calendar.

July						
Sunday	Monday	Tuesday	Wednesday	Thursday	Friday	Saturday
		1	2	3	4	5
6	7	8	9	10	11	12
13	14	15	16	17	18	19
20	21	22	23	24	25	26
27	28	29	30	31		

This month of July has ______ Sundays in all.

Name: ______________________ Date: ______________

8. What is the time shown on the clock?

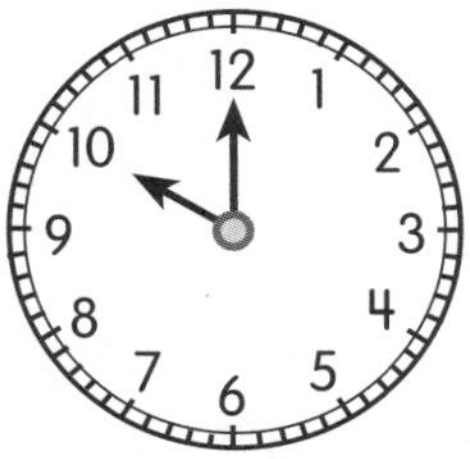

The time is ______________.

9. What is the time shown on the clock?

The time is ______________.

10. What is the time shown on the clock?

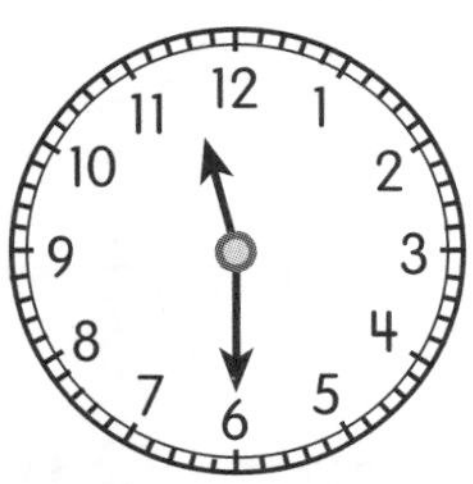

The time is ______________.

Name: ______________________ Date: ______________

Extended Response

(Question 11: 2 points, Questions 12 to 14: 3 x 1 point = 3 points)

11. Look at the calendar.
Find the mystery date.
The mystery date is on a Thursday.
After this date, there are three more Fridays left in the month.

September						
Sunday	**Monday**	**Tuesday**	**Wednesday**	**Thursday**	**Friday**	**Saturday**
			1	2	3	4
5	6	7	8	9	10	11
12	13	14	15	16	17	18
19	20	21	22	23	24	25
26	27	28	29	30		

The mystery date is ______________.

12. ______________ is the fourth day of the week.

13. Independence Day falls in the month of ______________.

14. ______________ is the season that comes before spring.

Name: ____________________ Date: ____________

Benchmark Assessment 2
for Chapters 10 to 15

/50

Suggested Time: 45 min

Multiple Choice

(10 x 2 points = 20 points)

Fill in the circle next to the correct answer.

1.

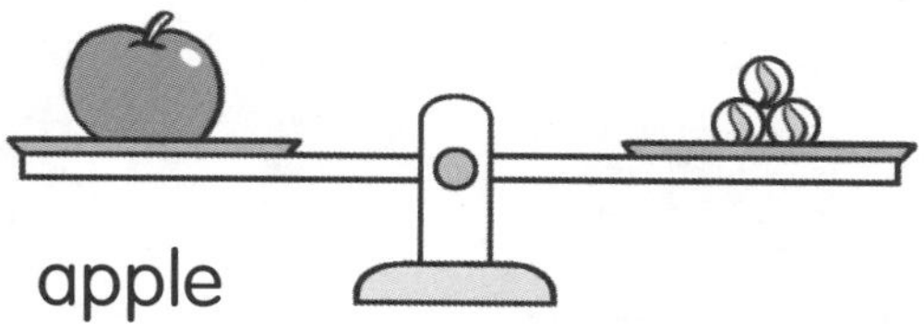

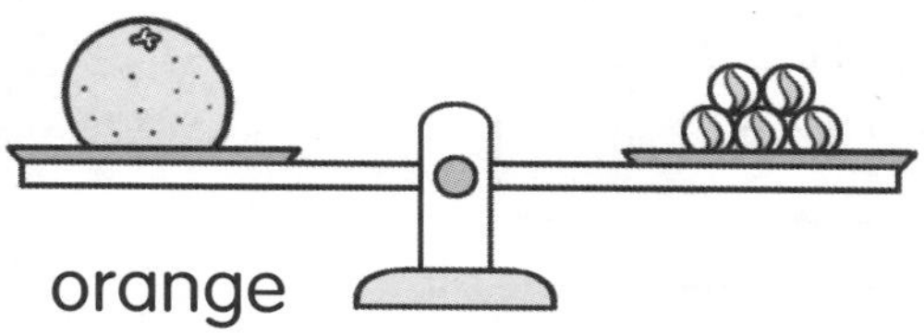

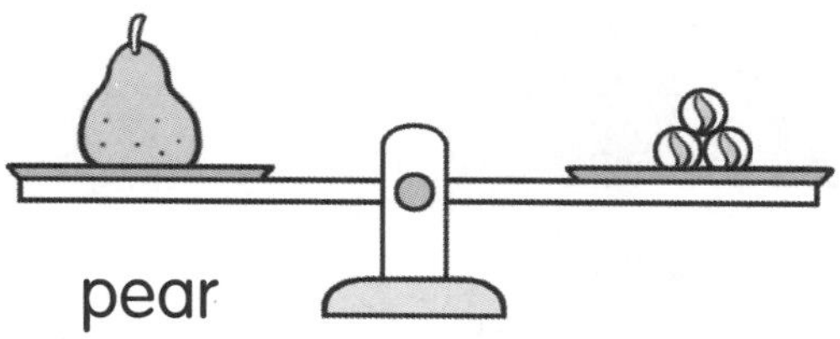

Which fruits have the same weight?

Ⓐ apple and orange
Ⓑ apple and pear
Ⓒ orange and pear
Ⓓ apple, orange, and pear

Name: ______________________________ Date: ______________

2. Which graph shows that there are more heads than tails when a coin is tossed 10 times?

Ⓐ

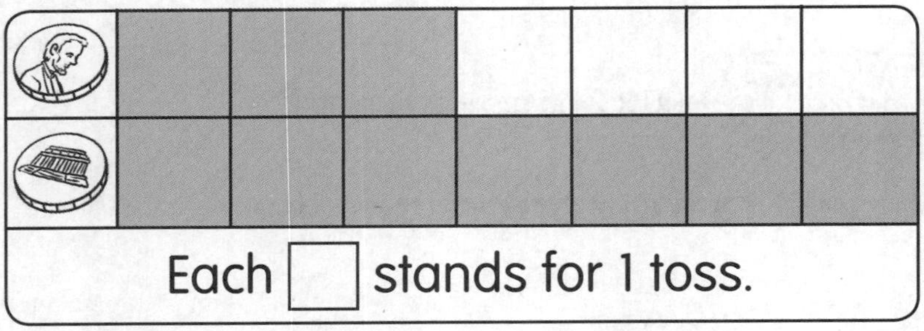

Ⓑ

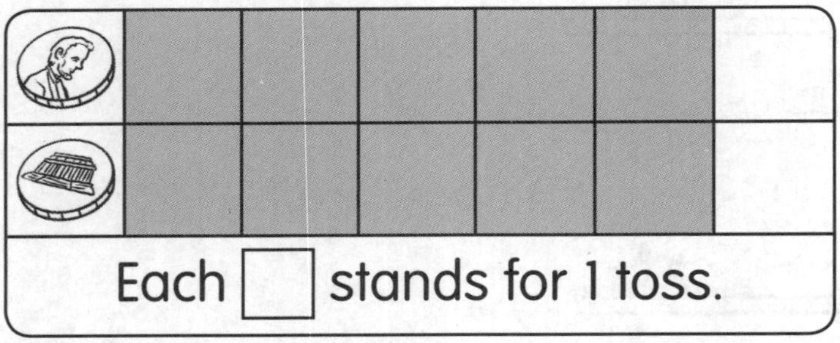

Ⓒ

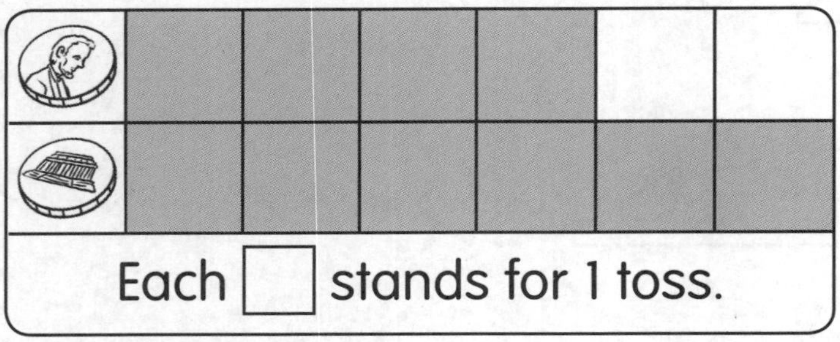

Ⓓ

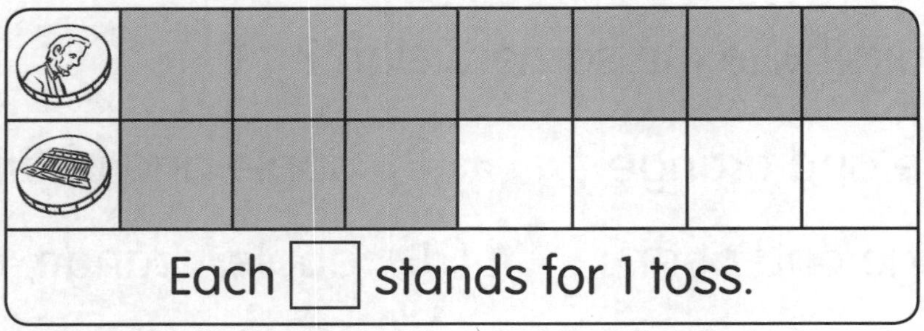

Name: ______________________ Date: ______________

3. Which number has 3 tens?

Ⓐ 3 Ⓑ 38 Ⓒ 13 Ⓓ 23

4. Add 3 + 9 + 8.

Ⓐ 10 Ⓑ 11 Ⓒ 17 Ⓓ 20

5. Subtract 17 from 35.

Ⓐ 18 Ⓑ 22 Ⓒ 28 Ⓓ 39

6. In which season is Halloween?

Ⓐ Spring Ⓑ Summer Ⓒ Winter Ⓓ Fall

7. How many marbles fewer is the weight of Book A than Book B?

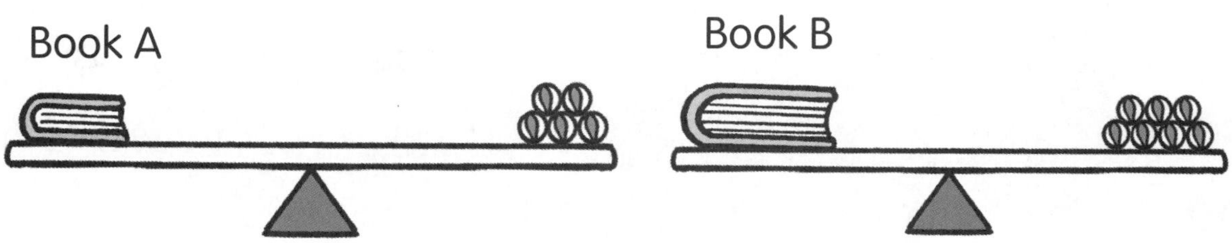

Ⓐ 2 Ⓑ 5 Ⓒ 7 Ⓓ 12

Name: ______________________________ Date: ______________

8. Look at the picture graph.
How many more children like bananas than apples?

Children's Favorite Fruits

Apple	● ● ● ● ● ●
Banana	● ● ● ● ● ● ●
Orange	● ● ●

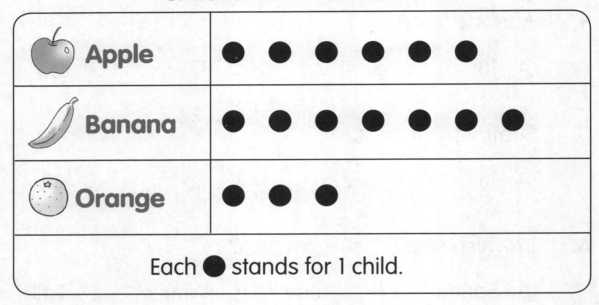

Each ● stands for 1 child.

Ⓐ 1 Ⓑ 2 Ⓒ 4 Ⓓ 5

9. What is the same as 3 tens 8 ones?

Ⓐ 5 Ⓑ 11 Ⓒ 24 Ⓓ 38

10. Which clock shows half past 12?

Ⓐ

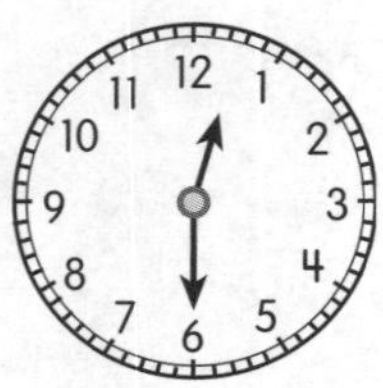

Ⓑ

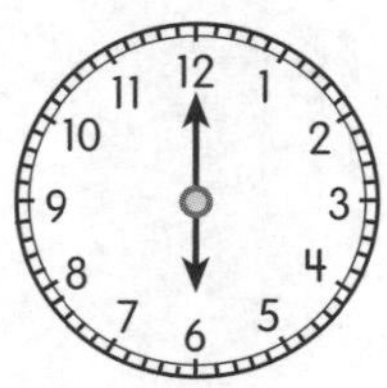

Ⓒ

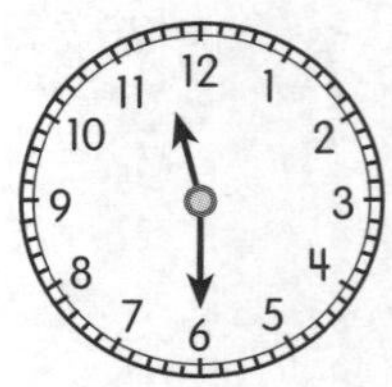

Ⓓ

Name: ______________________ Date: ______________

Short Answer

(10 x 2 points = 20 points)

Follow the directions.

11. The graph shows the number of stickers each friend has.

Number of Stickers

What is the difference between the most and fewest stickers? ______

Name: ______________________ Date: ____________

12. Look at the picture.
Fill in the blanks.

The ____________ is heavier than the ____________.

13. Complete the number pattern.

16, 19, 22, ________, ________

14. Three days after Thursday is ____________.

15. What is the time shown on the clock?

The time is ____________.

Name: ______________________ Date: ____________

16. Cindy has read 21 pages of a book. She has 19 more pages left to read. How many pages are there in the book?

There are ______ pages in the book.

17. Sharon needs 35 cards to play a game. She already has 27 cards. How many more cards does she need?

She needs ______ more cards.

18. Add.

$$\begin{array}{r} 16 \\ +\ 24 \\ \hline \end{array}$$

Name: ______________________ Date: ____________

19. Each  stands for 1 unit.

watermelon

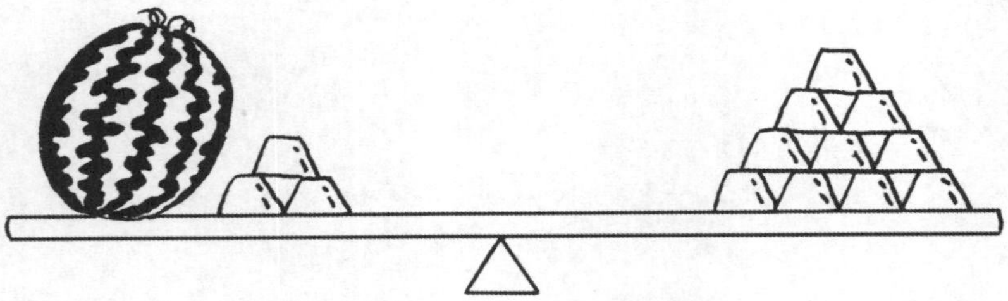

The watermelon has a weight of _______ units.

20. Look at the bar graph.

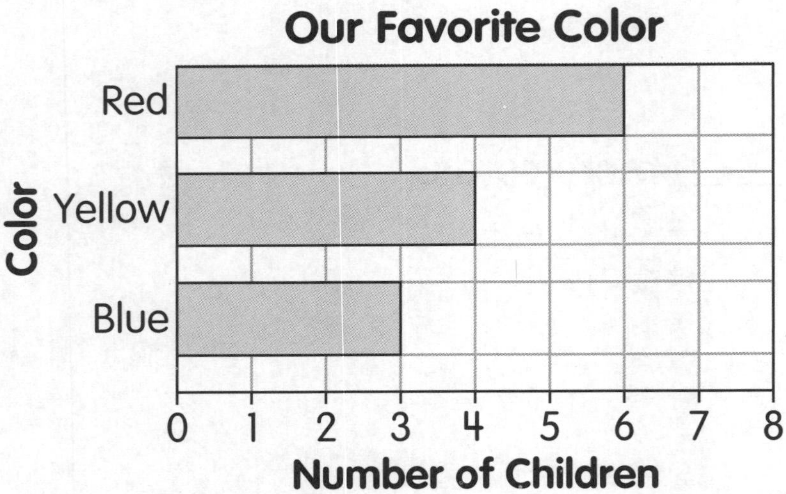

How many children like red or yellow? _______

Name: ______________________ Date: ______________

Extended Response

(Question 21: 3 points, Question 22: 4 points, Question 23 to 25: 3 x 1 point = 3 points)

Solve.
Show your work.

21. Mary has 24 seashells.
Alex has 8 fewer seashells than Mary.
How many seashells does Alex have?

Alex has ______ seashells.

22. Joe had some crayons.
He gave 5 crayons to his cousin and 9 crayons to his sister.
Joe has 9 crayons left.
How many crayons did Joe have at first?

Joe had ______ crayons at first.

Name: ______________________________ Date: ______________

Look at the weight of the items below.
Fill in the blanks.

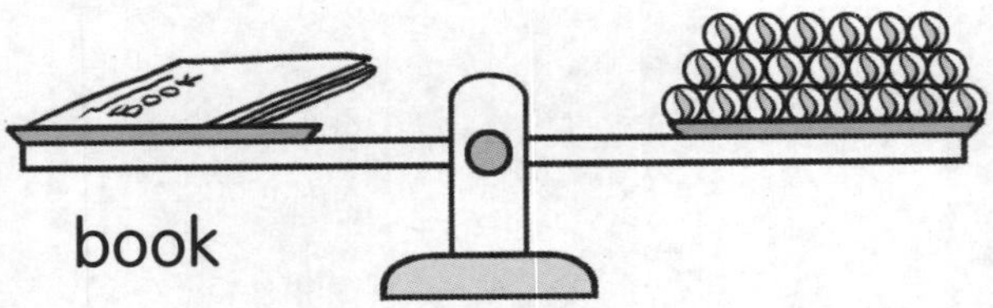

book

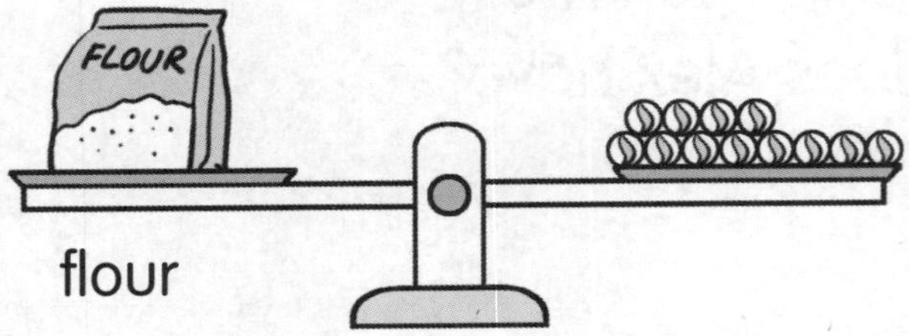

flour

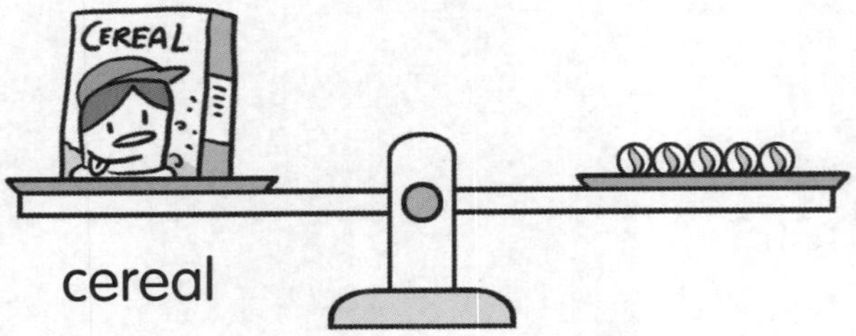

cereal

23. The weight of the bag of flour is _______ marbles.

24. The _______ is the heaviest.

25. The book is _______ marbles heavier than the box of cereal.

Name: ______________________ Date: ______________

Bonus Questions

Follow the directions.

1. Look at the pictures.
Which box is the lightest?

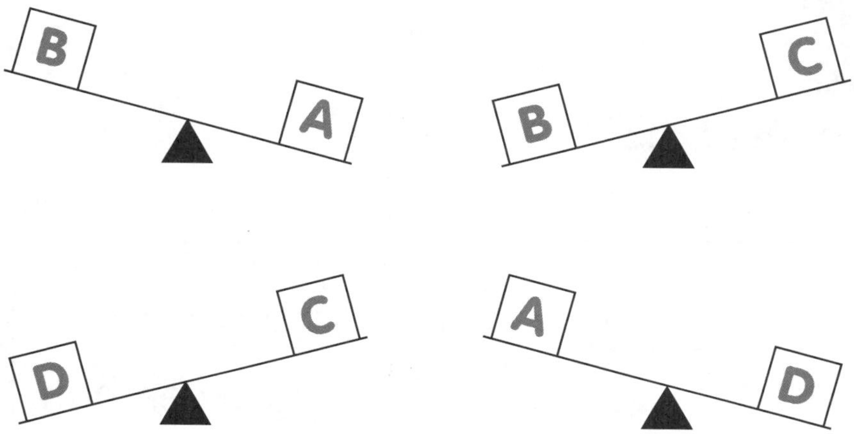

Box ________ is the lightest.

Fill in the missing numbers.

2.

$$\begin{array}{r} \square\ 6 \\ +\ 2\ \square \\ \hline 4\ 0 \end{array}$$

3.

$$\begin{array}{r} 3\ \square \\ -\ \square\ 7 \\ \hline 1\ 3 \end{array}$$

Name: ______________________ Date: ______________

PRE-TEST 16

Numbers to 100

Vocabulary

Fill in the blanks.
Use the words in the box.

make
less than
greater than

1. 33 is ______________ 28.

2. 29 is ______________ 31.

3. 25 and 5 ______________ 30.

Write the numbers in words.

4. 27 ______________

5. 39 ______________

Concepts and Skills

Fill in the blanks.

6. 3 more than 24 is ______.

7. 5 less than 34 is ______.

Name: ______________________ Date: ____________

8. ______ is 6 more than 27.

9. ______ is 4 less than 32.

Complete the number patterns.

10. 15, 19, 23, ______, 31, ______, 39

11. 38, ______, 28, 23, ______, 13, 8

Problem Solving

Compare.
Fill in the missing numbers.

25 19 32 21

12. The least number is ______.

13. ______ is greater than 25.

14. ______ is less than 25 but greater than 19.

15. Order the numbers from least to greatest.

______, ______, ______, ______
least

Name: ______________________ Date: ______________

16 Numbers to 100

TEST PREP

25
Suggested Time: 30 min

Multiple Choice

(5 x 2 points = 10 points)

Fill in the circle next to the correct answer.

1. 76 69 98 89

Which is the greatest number?

Ⓐ 76 Ⓑ 69 Ⓒ 98 Ⓓ 89

2. Which number is between 89 and 91?

Ⓐ 88 Ⓑ 90 Ⓒ 92 Ⓓ 93

3. How many blocks are there?

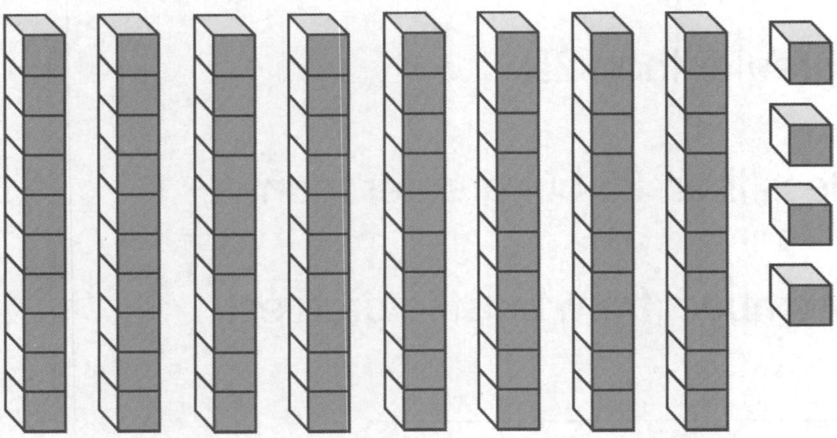

Ⓐ 60 + 4 = 64 Ⓑ 70 + 4 = 74

Ⓒ 80 + 4 = 84 Ⓓ 90 + 4 = 94

Name: ______________________ Date: ____________

4. Skip count by twos.
What are the missing numbers?

50, 52, ______, ______, ______, 60

Ⓐ 53, 55, 57

Ⓑ 54, 55, 58

Ⓒ 54, 56, 59

Ⓓ 54, 56, 58

5. What is 2 tens more than 80?

Ⓐ 60 Ⓑ 78 Ⓒ 82 Ⓓ 100

Short Answer
(5 x 2 points = 10 points)

Follow the directions.

6. Write the number in the box.

sixty-nine	

7. Fill in the missing number.

5 tens and 9 ones is the same as ______.

8. Fill in the place-value chart.

47 =

Tens	Ones

Name: ______________________ Date: ______________

9. Write the missing number on the number line.

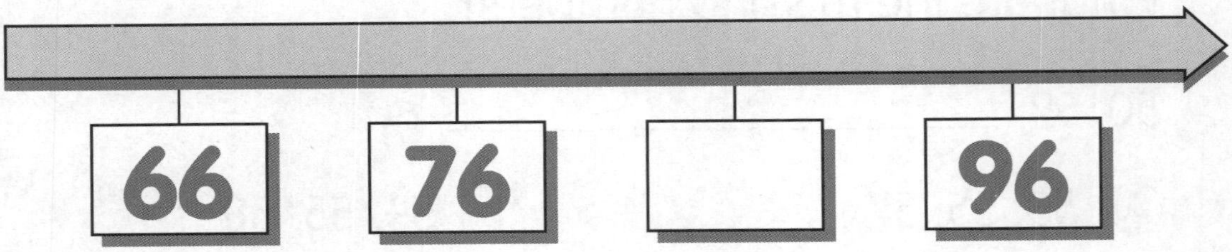

10. Fill in the missing number.

_______ and 9 make 79.

Extended Response

(Questions 11 to 13: 3 x 1 point = 3 points, Question 14: 2 points)

Fill in the blanks.
Use the numbers in the pictures.

11. The least number is _______.

12. _______ is greater than 72 but less than 91.

13. 4 less than 72 is _______.

14. Order the numbers from greatest to least.

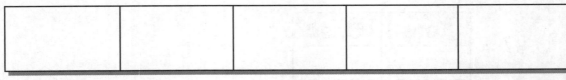

greatest

Name: ______________________ Date: ______________

PRE-TEST 17

Addition and Subtraction to 100

Vocabulary

Fill in the missing words.

count backward	counting on	regroup

1. We can add two numbers using the ______________ method.

2. We can ______________ 24 ones into 1 ten and 14 ones.

3. We ______________ from the greater number when we subtract.

Concepts and Skills

Add or subtract.

4. 22 + 15 = ________

5. 15 + 8 = ________

6. 28 – 6 = ________

Name: ____________________ Date: ____________

7. $35 - 9 =$ ______

8. $31 - 14 =$ ______

Problem Solving

Solve.
Show your work.

9. Luke drives 18 miles in the morning.
He drives 6 miles less in the morning than in the afternoon.
How many miles does Luke drive in the afternoon?

☐ ◯ ☐ = ☐

Luke drives ______ miles in the afternoon.

10. There are 18 tomatoes and 25 potatoes in a basket.
How many more potatoes than tomatoes are in the basket?

☐ ◯ ☐ = ☐

There are ______ more potatoes.

Name: ______________________ Date: ______________

TEST PREP 17

Addition and Subtraction to 100

25
Suggested Time: 30 min

Multiple Choice

(5 x 2 points = 10 points)

Fill in the circle next to the correct answer.

1. 35 + 15 = ______ tens

Ⓐ 50 Ⓑ 40 Ⓒ 5 Ⓓ 4

2. 39 + 34 = ______ + 3

Ⓐ 6 ones Ⓑ 7 ones Ⓒ 6 tens Ⓓ 7 tens

3. Add.

$$\begin{array}{r} 5\,2 \\ +\quad 3 \\ \hline \end{array}$$

Ⓐ 45 Ⓑ 46 Ⓒ 55 Ⓓ 56

4. Subtract 13 from 68.
What is the answer?

Ⓐ 55 Ⓑ 65 Ⓒ 71 Ⓓ 81

Name: ______________________ Date: ______________

5. $62 - 9 =$ ______

Ⓐ 17 Ⓑ 35 Ⓒ 53 Ⓓ 71

Short Answer

(5 x 2 points = 10 points)

Follow the directions.

6. Fill in the missing number.

$5 + 85 =$ ______ tens

7. Fill in the missing number.

$77 -$ ______ $= 71$

8. Fill in the missing number.

$64 +$ ______ $= 81$

9. Add.

$$\begin{array}{r} 32 \\ +\ 59 \\ \hline \end{array}$$

Name: ______________________ Date: ______________

10. Subtract.

$$\begin{array}{r} 84 \\ -\ 15 \\ \hline \end{array}$$

Extended Response

(Question 11: 2 points, Question 12: 3 points)

Solve.
Show your work.

11. 32 children are in the library.
25 more children join them.
How many children are in the library now?

☐ ○ ☐ = ☐

_______ children are in the library now.

12. Mr. Richards has 76 apples in a basket.
He has 35 fewer oranges than apples.
How many oranges does Mr. Richards have?

☐ ○ ☐ = ☐

Mr. Richards has _______ oranges.

Name: ______________________ Date: ____________

PRE-TEST 18 Multiplication and Division

Vocabulary

Fill in the blanks.
Use the words in the box.

doubles fact	add	make

1. 5 and 5 ____________ 10.

2. 3 + 3 is a ____________.

3. Plus means to ____________.

Concepts and Skills

Add.

4. 8 + 8 = ______

5. 7 + 7 + 7 = ______

6. 4 + 4 + 4 + 4 = ______

7. 5 + 5 + 5 + 5 + 5 = ______

Name: ____________________ Date: __________

Complete the number patterns.

8. 2, 4, 6, ______, 10, ______, 14

9. 5, 10, ______, 20, 25, ______, 35

10. 10, ______, 30, 40, ______, 60

Problem Solving

Solve.
Show your work.

11. Katie has 4 pencils.
Mark gives her 4 pencils.
How many pencils does Katie have in all?

☐ ○ ☐ = ☐

Katie has ______ pencils in all.

12. 9 boys are reading.
9 girls join them.
How many children are reading in all?

☐ ○ ☐ = ☐

There are ______ children reading in all.

Name: ______________________ Date: ____________

TEST PREP 18 Multiplication and Division

/ 25

Suggested Time: 30 min

Multiple Choice

(5 x 2 points = 10 points)

Fill in the circle next to the correct answer.

1. 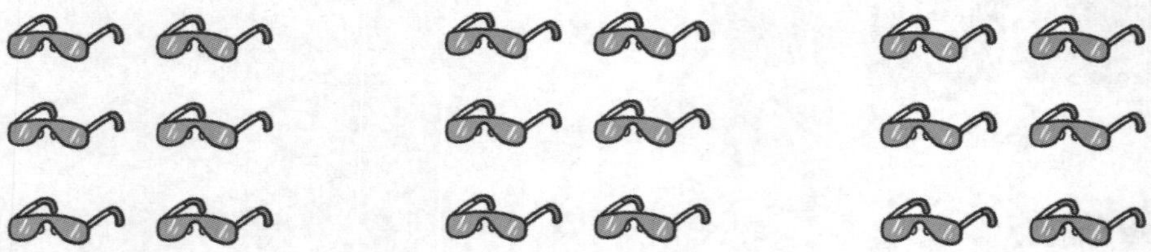

The picture shows ____________.

Ⓐ 6 groups of 3 Ⓑ 6 groups of 6

Ⓒ 3 groups of 6 Ⓓ 3 groups of 3

2. 5 groups of 4 = ____________.

Ⓐ 5 x 5 x 5 x 5 Ⓑ 4 x 4 x 4 x 4 x 4

Ⓒ 4 + 4 + 4 + 4 + 4 Ⓓ 5 + 5 + 5 + 5 + 5

3. Which number is equal to 5 threes?

Ⓐ 5 Ⓑ 10 Ⓒ 15 Ⓓ 20

Name: ______________________ Date: ______________

4. Mary has 16 tops.
She puts 2 tops into each box.
How many boxes does Mary need?

Ⓐ 8 Ⓑ 14 Ⓒ 18 Ⓓ 32

5. Mr. Mohan has 20 guitars in his shop.
He places 4 guitars on each shelf.
How many shelves does Mr. Mohan need?

Ⓐ 4 Ⓑ 5 Ⓒ 16 Ⓓ 24

Name: ______________________ Date: ______________

Short Answer

(5 x 2 points = 10 points)

Follow the directions.

6. Sally has 3 bags.
She puts 5 apples into each bag.

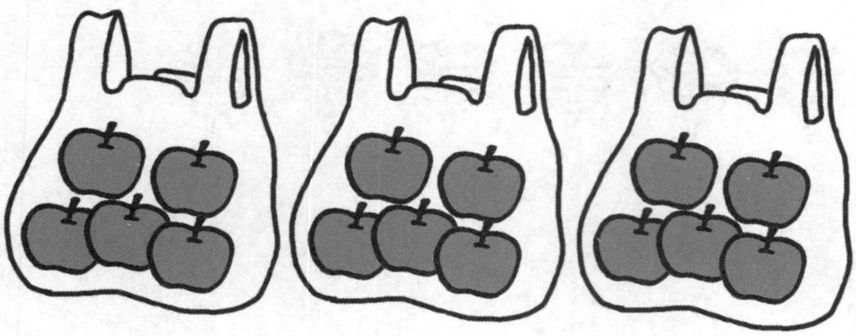

3 fives = ______ + ______ + ______

Sally has ______ apples in all.

7. Andy has 4 kittens.
Each kitten has 4 legs.

4 fours = ______ + ______ + ______ + ______

The kittens have ______ legs in all.

Name: ______________________ Date: ______________

8. Shirley puts 12 cartons of milk equally into 4 bags.

She puts ______ cartons of milk into each bag.

9. Circle groups of 5.
How many groups are there?

There are ______ groups of 5 apples.

Name: ______________________ Date: ______________

10. David has 16 glasses.
He places 4 glasses on each tray.
How many trays does David need?

David needs ______ trays.

Extended Response

(Question 11: 2 points, Question 12: 3 points)

Solve.
Show your work.

11. There are 8 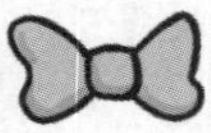 altogether.

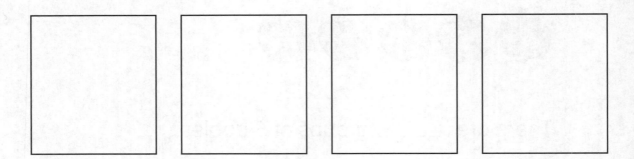

Draw an equal number of 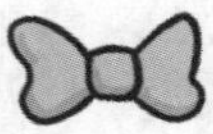 in each box.

Name: ______________________ Date: ______________

12. Mandy has 4 boxes of markers.
Each box has 3 markers.
How many markers does Mandy have in all?

☐ ○ ☐ ○ ☐ ○ ☐ = ☐

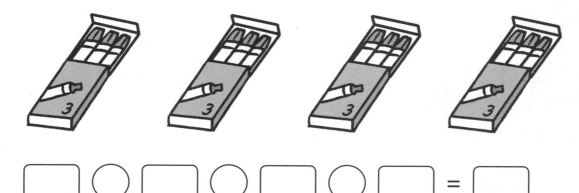

Mandy has ______ markers in all.

Name: ______________________ Date: ______________

PRE-TEST 19 Money

Vocabulary

Match the coins to the names.

1.  ● ● dime

2.  ● ● nickel

3.  ● ● penny

Concepts and Skills

Count the money.
Write the amount.

4. 

______ cents

Name: ______________________________ Date: ______________

5.

_______ cents

6.

_______ cents

Problem Solving

Circle the coins needed to pay for the things.

7.

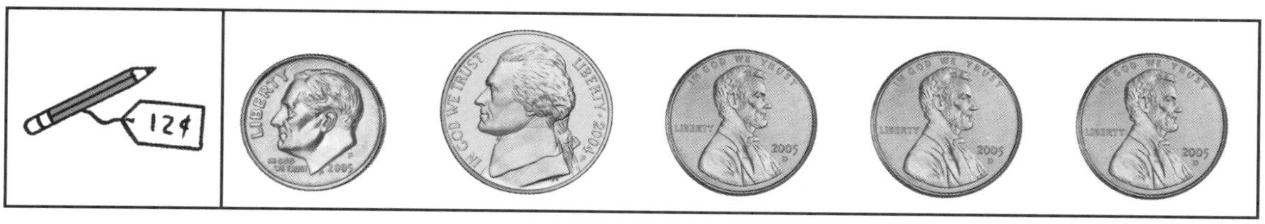

8.

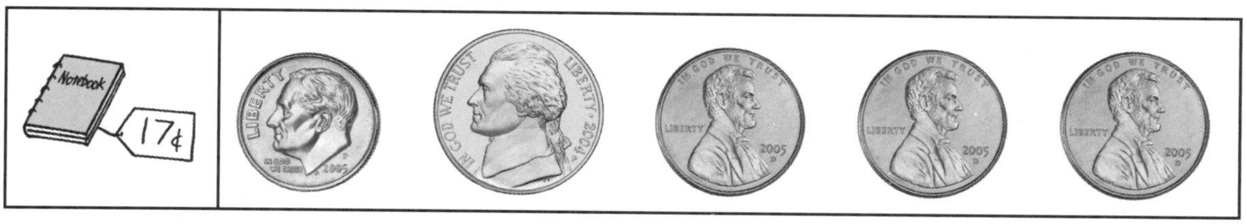

Name: ______________________ Date: ______________

TEST PREP 19 Money

	25
Suggested Time: 30 min	

Multiple Choice
(5 x 2 points = 10 points)

Fill in the circle next to the correct answer.

1. What is the value of these coins?

Ⓐ 5¢ Ⓑ 17¢ Ⓒ 23¢ Ⓓ 25¢

2. Which combination of coins shows 21¢?

Ⓐ 

Ⓑ 

Ⓒ 

Ⓓ 

Name: ______________________ Date: ______________

3. Tania has three coins.
She has 12¢.
Which three coins could Tania have?

Ⓐ 1 penny and 2 nickel

Ⓑ 1 nickel and 2 pennies

Ⓒ 1 dime and 2 pennies

Ⓓ 1 penny, 1 dime, and 1 nickel

4. Zack has 1 quarter, 1 dime, 3 nickels, and 7 pennies.
Which toy can he buy?

Ⓐ

Ⓑ

Ⓒ

Ⓓ

Name: ______________________ Date: ______________

5. Which group of coins has the same value as 1 quarter and 3 dimes?

Ⓐ 1 quarter and 5 nickels

Ⓑ 2 quarters and 1 nickel

Ⓒ 1 quarter and 5 pennies

Ⓓ 1 quarter, 1 dime, and 3 nickels

Short Answer

(5 x 2 points = 10 points)

Follow the directions.

6. Karen has 16¢ in her pocket.
Which 3 coins could she have?
Circle the coins.

7. Alex buys a pen with the coins shown.
How much does the pen cost?

The pen costs ________¢.

Name: ______________________ Date: ______________

8. Fill in the blank.

2 quarters = ______ dimes

9. Larry has 2 quarters, 1 nickel, and 6 pennies.
How much money does he have?

He has ______¢.

10.

Ally has these coins.
She wants to buy a muffin.
The muffin costs 50¢.
How much more money does Ally need?

Ally needs ______¢ more.

Name: ______________________ Date: ______________

Extended Response

(Question 11: 2 points, Question 12: 3 points)

Solve.
Show your work.

11. Kim bought a notebook and a pencil.
How much did Kim spend on these two items?

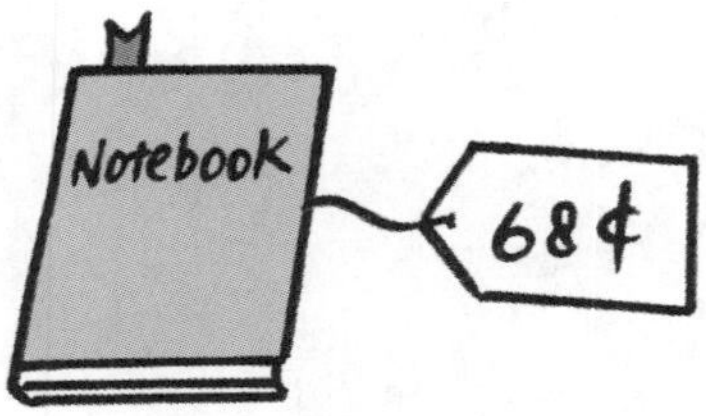

She spent ______¢ for the two items.

12. Jen buys a sticker for 58¢.
She pays for it with 2 quarters, a nickel,
and some pennies.
How many pennies does Jen use?

Jen uses ______ pennies.

Name: ______________________ Date: ____________

End-of-Year Test

100
Suggested Time: 1½ hour

Multiple Choice

(20 x 2 points = 40 points)

Fill in the circle next to the correct answer.

1. What number is greater than 6 but less than 8?

Ⓐ 5 Ⓑ 7 Ⓒ 8 Ⓓ 9

2. What number and 2 make 7?

Ⓐ 3 Ⓑ 4 Ⓒ 5 Ⓓ 9

3. 1 + 2 = 

What is  + ?

Ⓐ 3 Ⓑ 4 Ⓒ 6 Ⓓ 9

4. Find the missing number.

☐ − 2 = 7

Ⓐ 5 Ⓑ 7 Ⓒ 8 Ⓓ 9

Name: ______________________ Date: ______________

5. Complete the pattern.

Ⓐ 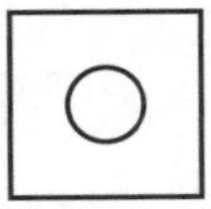 Ⓑ 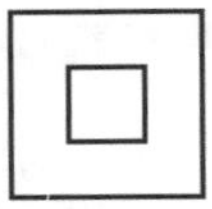 Ⓒ 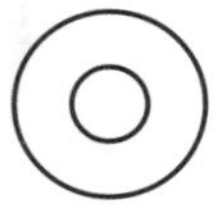 Ⓓ 

6. Look at the numbers.

Add 5 to the 2nd number from the left.
What is the answer?

Ⓐ 23 Ⓑ 26 Ⓒ 39 Ⓓ 45

7. Keagan has 20 fish.
He has 6 fewer snails than fish.
How many snails does Keagan have?

Ⓐ 14 Ⓑ 26 Ⓒ 34 Ⓓ 46

8. 2 tens = ☐ + 16
What is ☐?

Ⓐ 4 Ⓑ 14 Ⓒ 18 Ⓓ 36

Name: ______________________ Date: ____________

9. Look at the picture.
Four kangaroos jumped to new spots
from points 1, 2, 3, and 4.
Which kangaroo made the farthest jump?

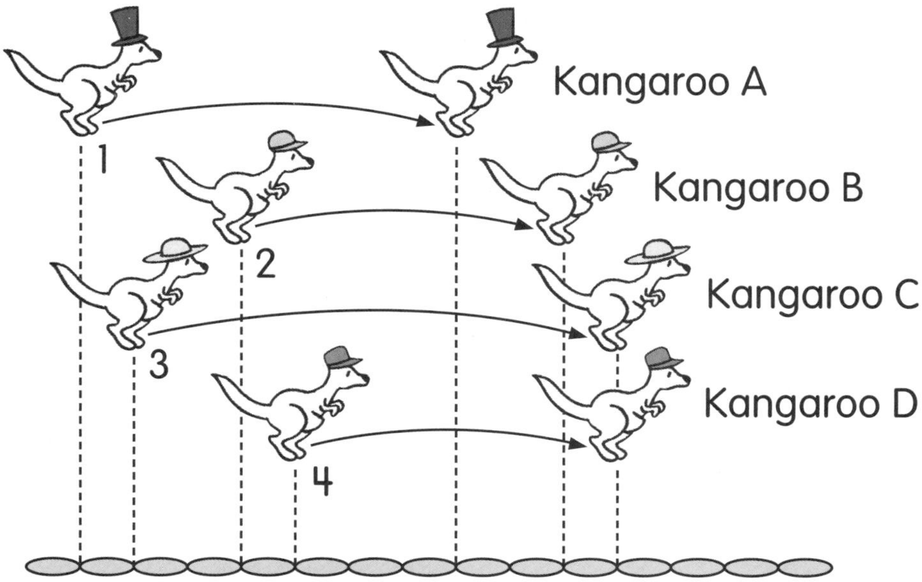

Ⓐ Kangaroo A Ⓑ Kangaroo B

Ⓒ Kangaroo C Ⓓ Kangaroo D

Name: ______________________ Date: ______________

10. Look at the picture.
Which animal is the lightest?

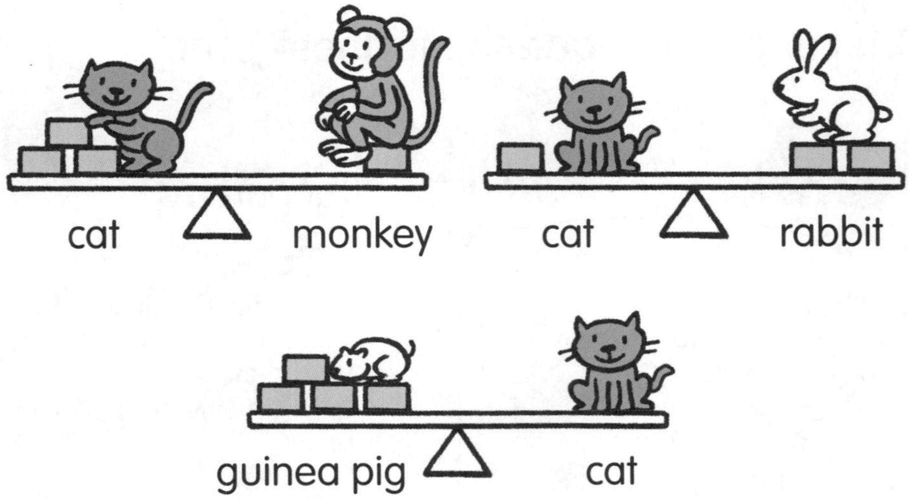

Ⓐ cat Ⓑ monkey

Ⓒ guinea pig Ⓓ rabbit

11. Look at the picture graph.
How many more children like apples than pears?

Children's Favorite Fruits

Apple	♥ ♥ ♥ ♥ ♥ ♥ ♥ ♥ ♥
Pear	♥ ♥ ♥ ♥ ♥
Strawberry	♥ ♥ ♥ ♥ ♥ ♥ ♥
Each ♥ stands for 1 child.	

Ⓐ 4 Ⓑ 5 Ⓒ 9 Ⓓ 14

Name: ______________________ Date: ____________

12. What is **not** the same as 3 tens 7 ones?

Ⓐ 3 + 7　　Ⓑ 30 + 7

Ⓒ thirty-seven　　Ⓓ 37

13. Which is least?

Ⓐ 29 – 5　　Ⓑ 28 – 6　　Ⓒ 21 + 2　　Ⓓ 18 + 3

14. What is 35 – 7?

Ⓐ 25　　Ⓑ 28　　Ⓒ 32　　Ⓓ 42

15. The clock shows the time Kenny's computer class starts. What time does Kenny's computer class start?

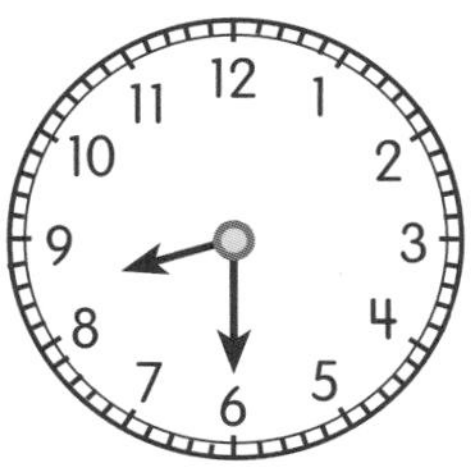

Ⓐ 8 o'clock　　Ⓑ half past 8

Ⓒ 12 o'clock　　Ⓓ half past 12

16. What is the same as 3 tens 17 ones?

Ⓐ 20　　Ⓑ 27　　Ⓒ 37　　Ⓓ 47

Name: ______________________ Date: ______________

17. 6 tens –  = 7

What is 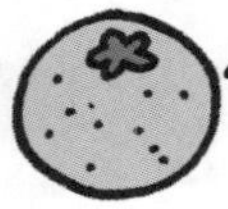?

Ⓐ 1 Ⓑ 13 Ⓒ 53 Ⓓ 57

18. What is **not** equal to 16?

Ⓐ 8 + 8 Ⓑ 4 + 4 + 4 + 4

Ⓒ 4 fours Ⓓ 2 fours

19. There are 18 slices of watermelon.
9 children share the slices of watermelon.
Each child gets an equal number of slices.
How many slices of watermelon does each child get?

Ⓐ 2 Ⓑ 3 Ⓒ 6 Ⓓ 9

Name: ______________________ Date: ______________

20. What is the value of these coins?

Ⓐ 12¢ Ⓑ 16¢ Ⓒ 20¢ Ⓓ 25¢

Short Answer

(20 x 2 points = 40 points)

Follow the directions.

21. Look at the picture.
Count the apples and pears.

apples pears

There are ______ more apples than pears.

22. Complete the number bond.

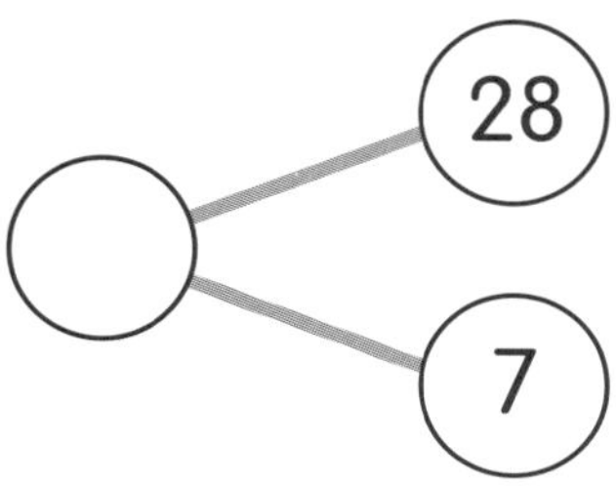

Name: ______________________________ Date: ______________

23. Look at the picture.
Write an addition sentence.

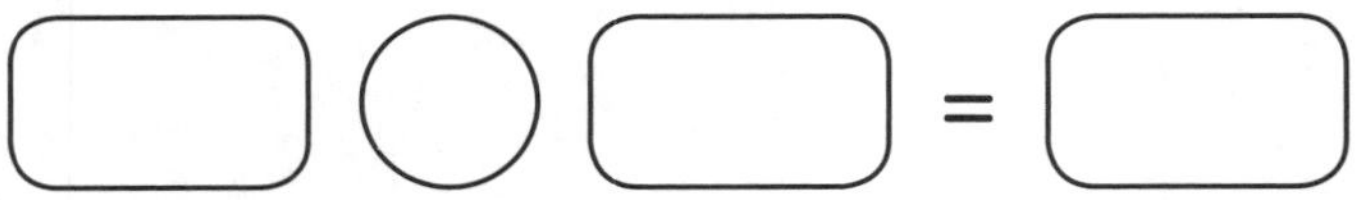

24. Fill in the blank.

_______ – 2 = 8

25. Draw the next shape.

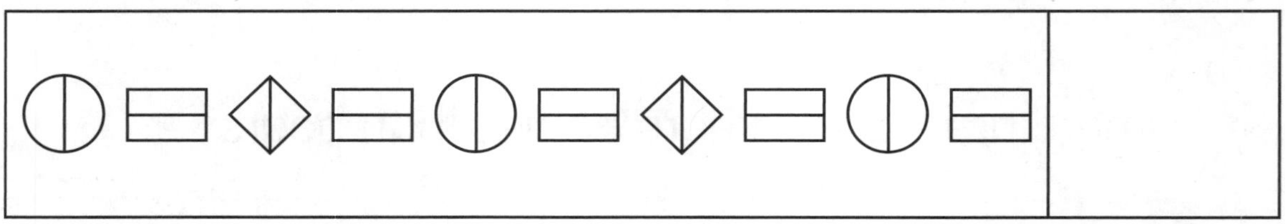

26. Draw a pair of ears on the third rabbit from the left.

Name: ______________________ Date: ______________

27. Eighteen comes just after ____________.

28. Fill in the blank.

6 + 8 + ________ = 20

29. Look at the picture.
Which ribbon is shorter than Ribbon A but longer than Ribbon B?
Color the ribbon.

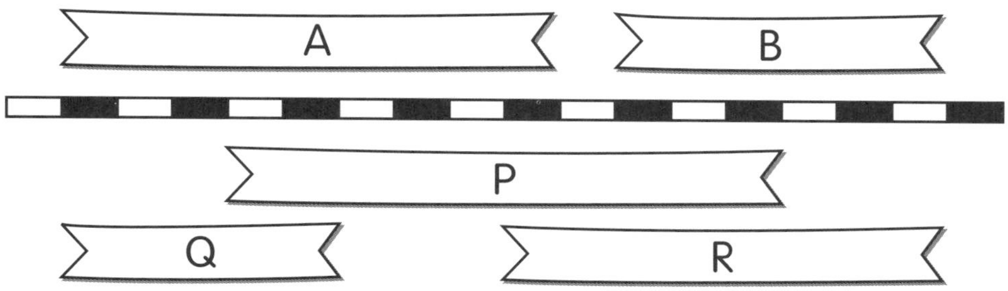

30.

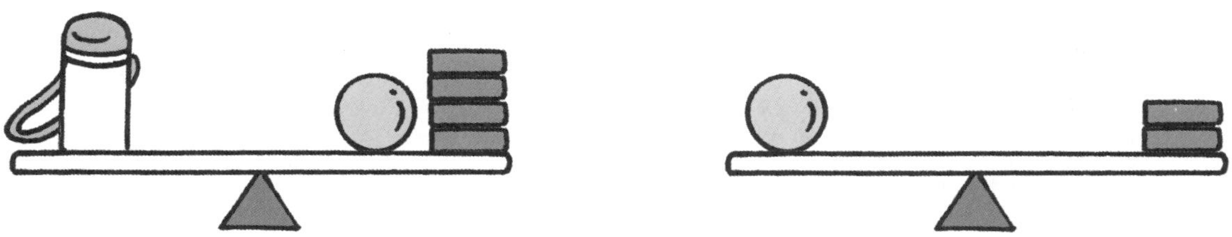

Each  stands for 1 wooden block.

The weight of the  is ________ wooden blocks.

Name: ______________________ Date: ______________

31. Look at the bar graph.

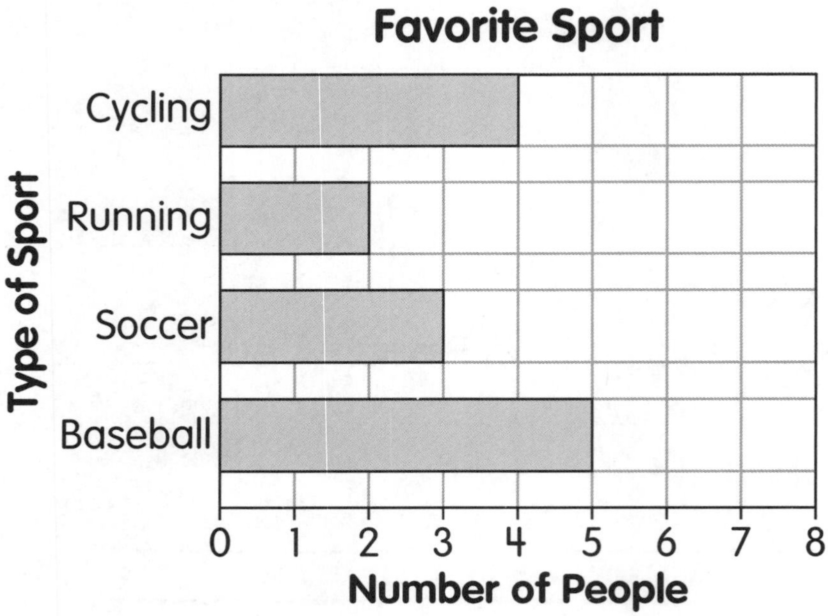

How many more people like baseball than running? ______

32. Write the number.

thirty-five	

33. Subtract.

$$\begin{array}{r} 31 \\ -\ 12 \\ \hline \end{array}$$

34. Fill in the blank.

38 + 23 = ______

Name: ______________________ Date: ______________

35. Look at the calendar.

May						
Sunday	Monday	Tuesday	Wednesday	Thursday	Friday	Saturday
	1	2	3	4	5	6
7	8	9	10	11	12	13
14	15	16	17	18	19	20
21	22	23	24	25	26	27
28	29	30	31			

The date of the first Sunday of May is ______.

36. 5 tens less than 90 = ______ tens

37. Add.

$$\begin{array}{r} 36 \\ +\ 47 \\ \hline \end{array}$$

38. Which flags give an answer of 36?
Color the correct flags.

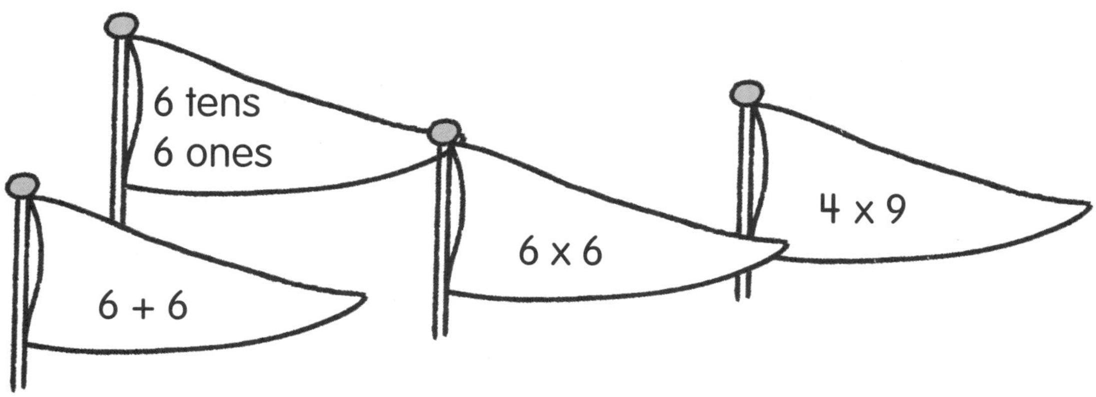

Name: ______________________ Date: ______________

39. Circle groups of airplanes to show 2 equal groups.

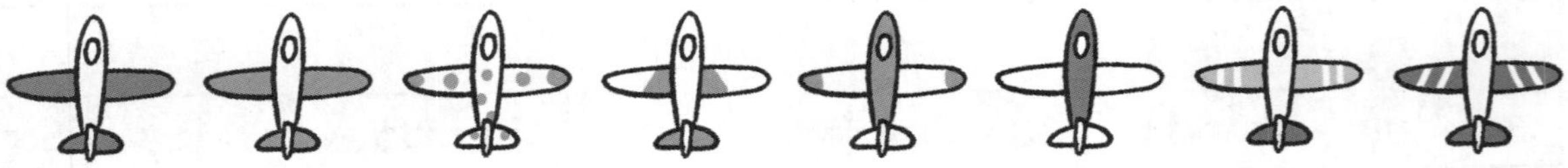

Each group has ______ airplanes in it.

40. Nick has these coins.
He wants to buy a pencil that costs 85¢.
How much more money does Nick need?

Nick needs ______¢ more.

Extended Response

(5 x 4 points = 20 points)

Solve.
Show your work.

41. Sally gives 3 hairclips to her sister.
She has 2 hairclips left.
How many hairclips did Sally have at first?

Sally had ______ hairclips at first.

Name: ______________________ Date: ______________

42. Aaron has 16 stickers.
Bob has 8 stickers more than Aaron.
How many stickers does Bob have?

Bob has ______ stickers.

43. A choir has 22 boys and 40 girls.
How many more girls than boys are in the choir?

______ more girls than boys are in the choir.

44. Mrs. Walker has 35 blue beads.
She has 29 yellow beads.
How many beads does Mrs. Walker have in all?

Mrs. Walker has ______ beads in all.

45. Gary has 3 quarters and 2 nickels.
He buys a snack that costs 82¢.
How much money does Gary have left?

Gary has ______¢ left.

Name: ______________________________ Date: ______________

Bonus Questions

Follow the directions.

1. Add.

$$\begin{array}{r} \square\ 2 \\ +\ \ 7\ \square \\ \hline \square\ 0\ 0 \end{array}$$

2. Subtract.

$$\begin{array}{r} 9\ \square \\ -\ \square\ 7 \\ \hline 5\ 6 \end{array}$$

3. Winnie has five coins.
The coins are worth 75¢.
What coins does Winnie have?
Circle the coins that Winnie has.

Answers

Pre-Test 1

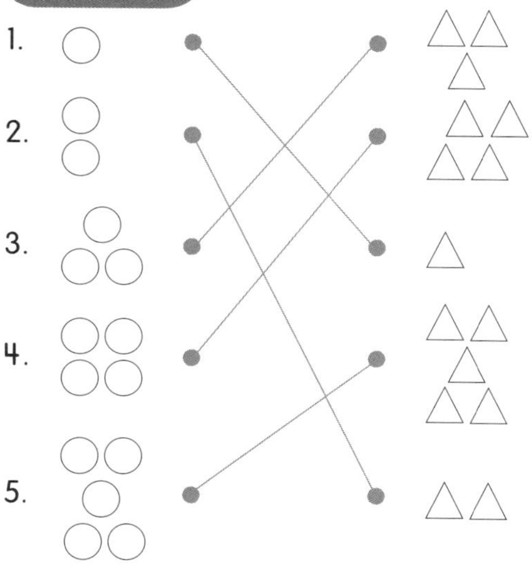

14. 0, 1, 2, 3, 4 [Answers vary]
15. 7, 8, 9, 10 [Answers vary]

Test Prep 1

1. C 2. D 3. B 4. D
5. A
6. 0
7. eight
8.

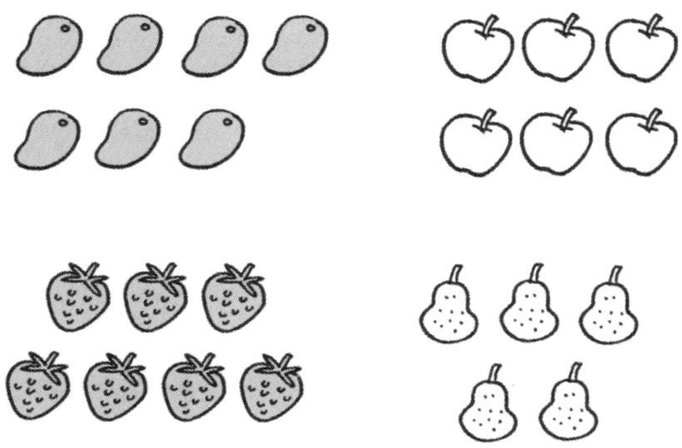

9.

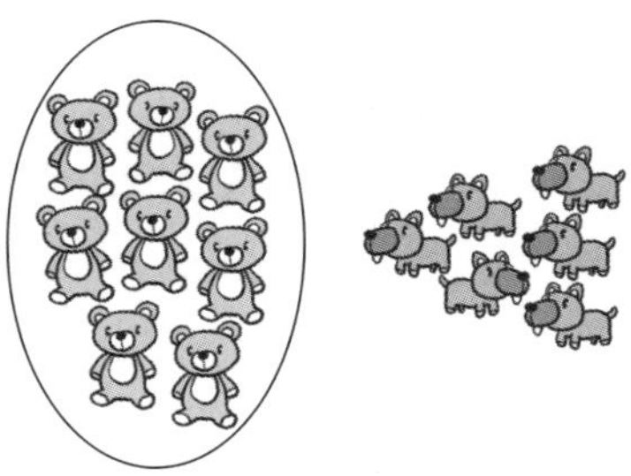

10. **10** 9 8 **7** 6 **5** 4
11. more
12. the same
13. fewer

Pre-Test 2

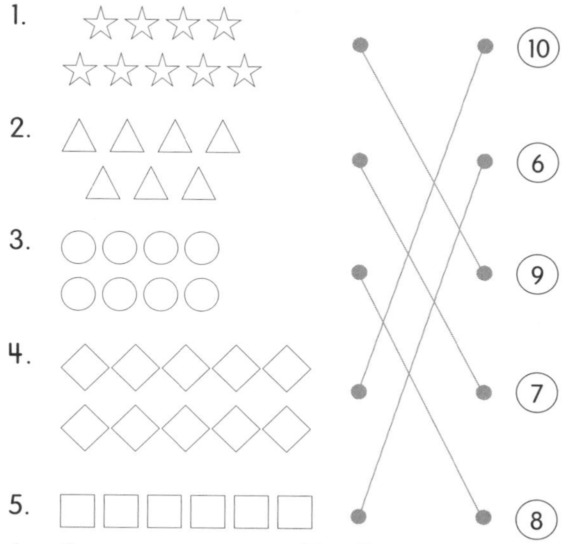

6. 9 7. 4
8. 4 9. 5
10. 1,
11. 2,
12. 3,
13. 4,
14. 5,
15. 6,
16. 7,
17. 8,
18. 9,
19. 10,

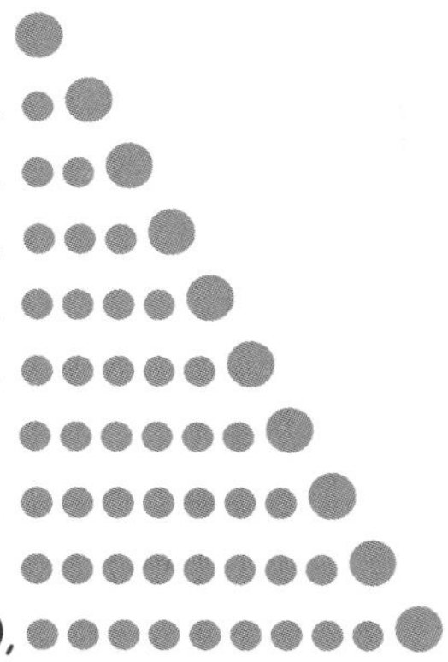

Test Prep 2

1. D 2. C 3. C 4. B
5. D
6.

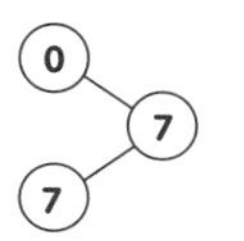

7. 2 (3) 5 (6) 8
8. 3
9.

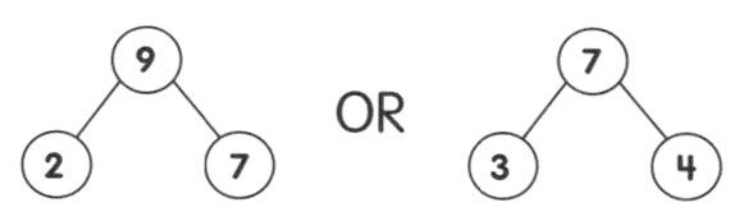

10. Answers vary.

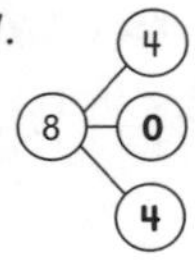

11.

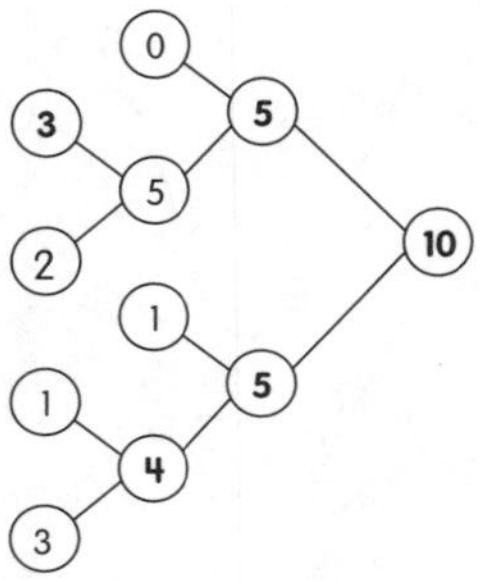

Pre-Test 3

1. less than
2. more than
3. less than
4. make
5. 10
6. 1
7. 6
8. 8
9.

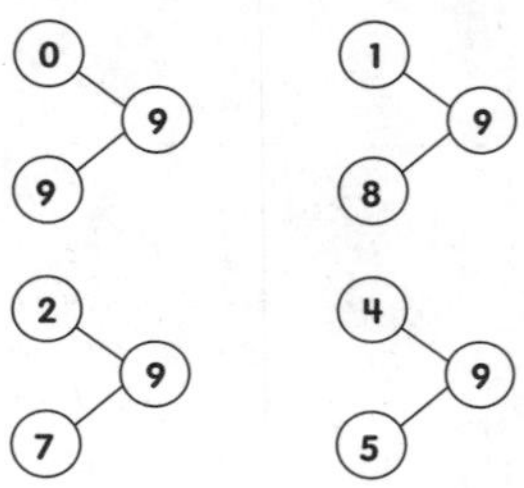

Test Prep 3

1. B
2. C
3. C
4. D
5. C
6. 4 + 2 = 6
7.

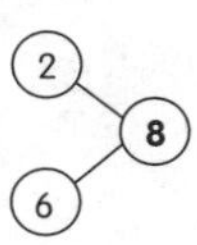

2 + 6 = 8

8.

9. 10
10. 6 + 3 = 9 OR 3 + 6 = 9
11. 5 + 2 = 7; 7
12.

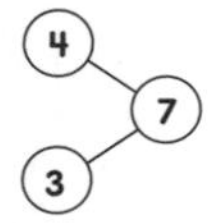

4 + 3 = 7
7

Pre-Test 4

1. more than
2. less than
3. equal to
4. less than
5. 4
6. 5
7. 5
8. 8
9.

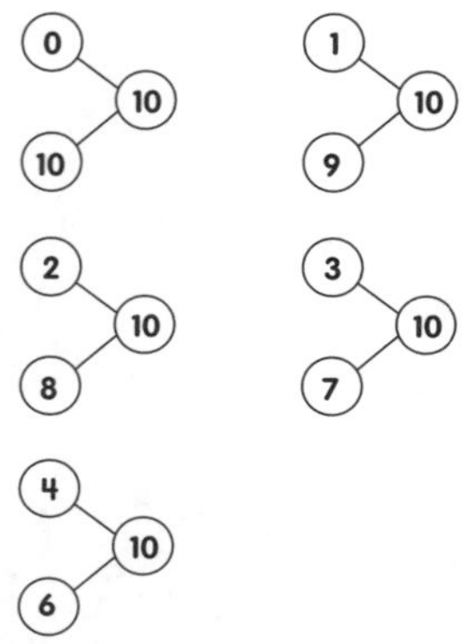

Test Prep 4

1. C
2. B
3. D
4. B
5. D
6. 6
7. 7 – 3 = 4 OR 7 – 4 = 3
8. 5
9.

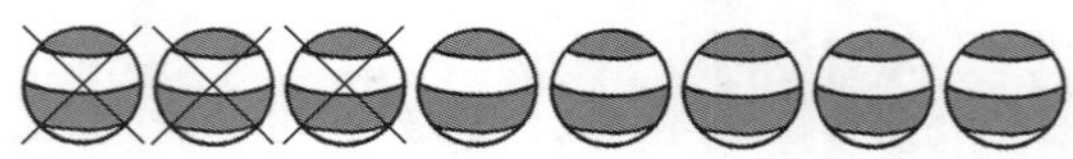

5

10. 2
11. 9 – 3 = 6; 6
12. 9; 9; 9

Benchmark Assessment 1

1. D
2. B
3. B
4. B
5. B
6. B
7. C
8. C
9. D
10. C
11. ten

12. 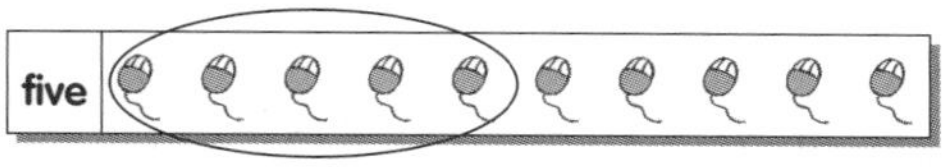

13. 

14.

0	**1**	2	3

15. Answers vary.

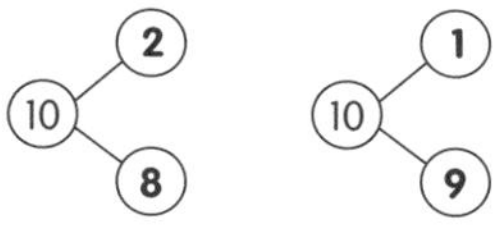

16. 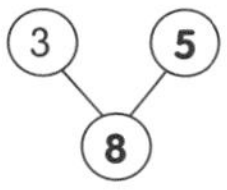

3 + 5 = 8

17. 7

18. 

19. 2

20. 6

21. 4 + 3 = 7; 7

22. 5 – 1 = 4; 4

23. 5 + 4 = 9; 9
9 – 2 = 7; 7

Bonus Questions

1. 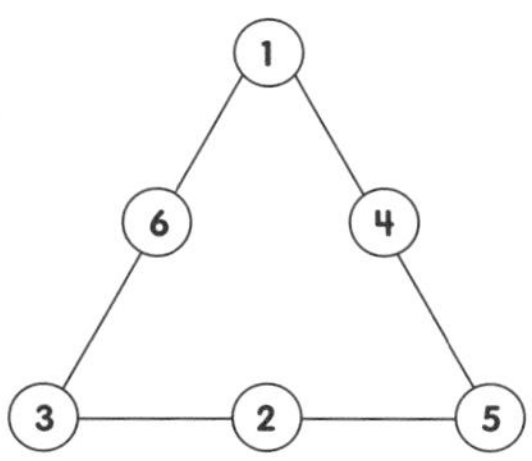

2. ♦ = **6** ♥ = **3**

3. 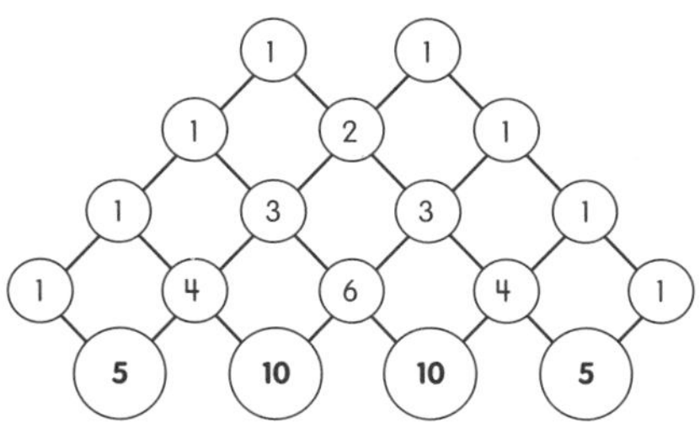

Pre-Test 5

1.–4. 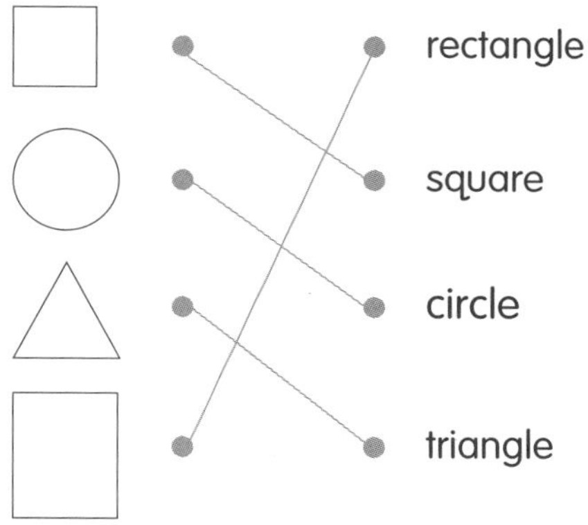

5.–8. 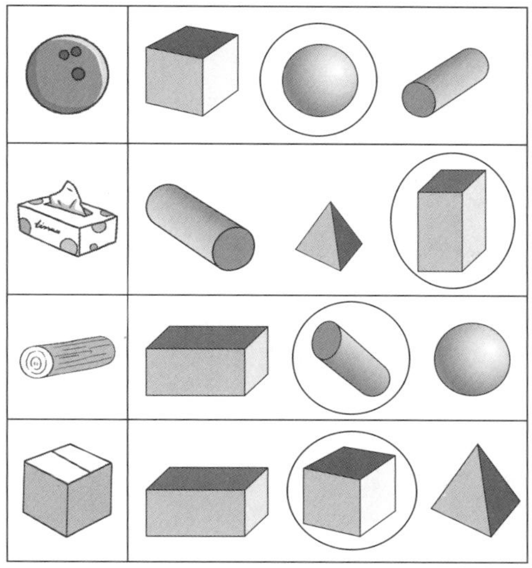

Test Prep 5

1. C 2. A 3. C 4. B

5. B

6. 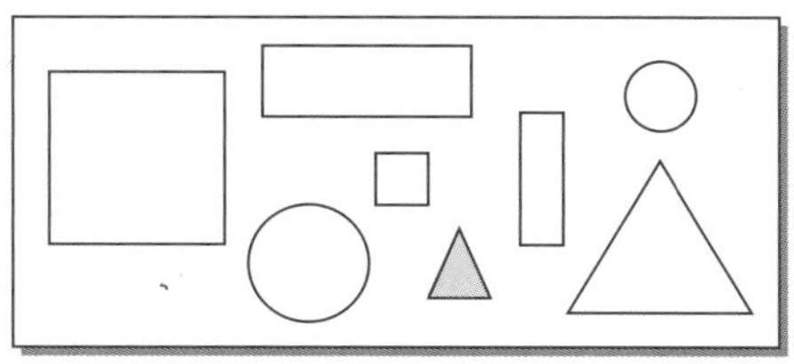

7. 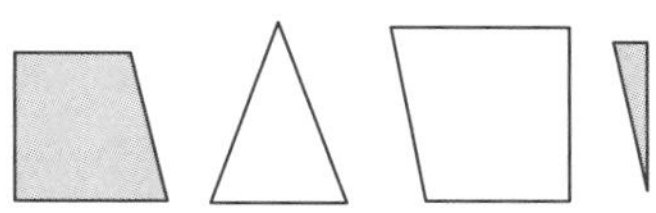

8. square

9. 

10. 

11. 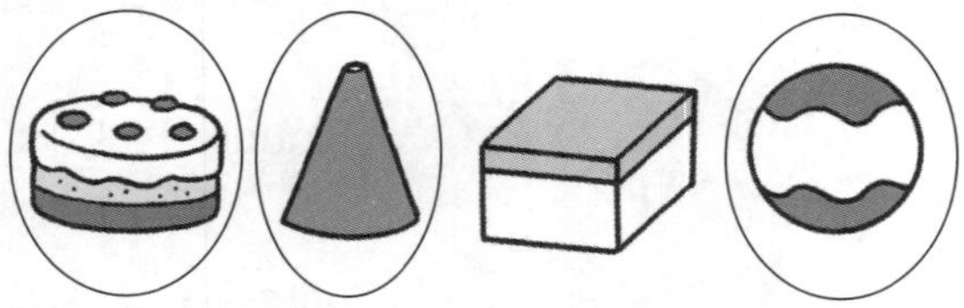

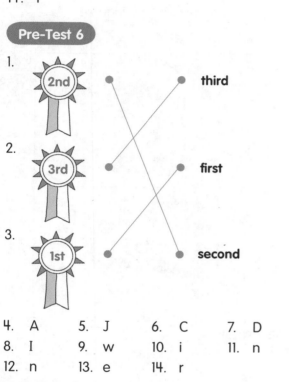

12. 3
13. 6
14. 4

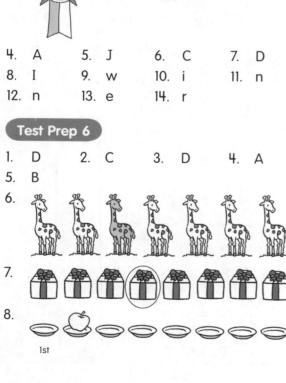

Pre-Test 6

1.
2.
3.

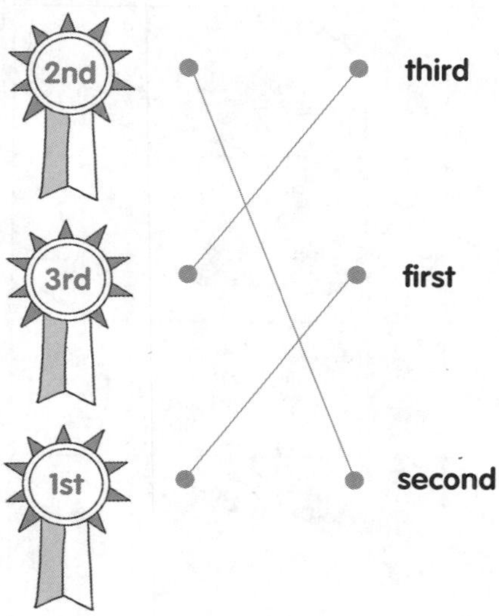

4. A
5. J
6. C
7. D
8. I
9. w
10. i
11. n
12. n
13. e
14. r

Test Prep 6

1. D
2. C
3. D
4. A
5. B
6. 
7. 
8. 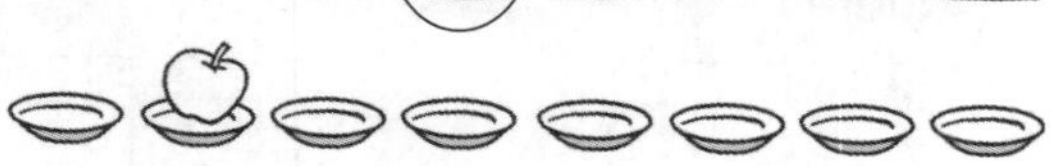

9. 

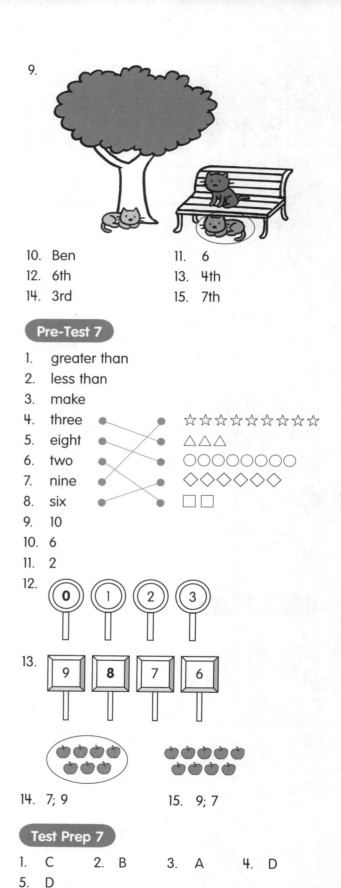

10. Ben
11. 6
12. 6th
13. 4th
14. 3rd
15. 7th

Pre-Test 7

1. greater than
2. less than
3. make
4. three
5. eight
6. two
7. nine
8. six

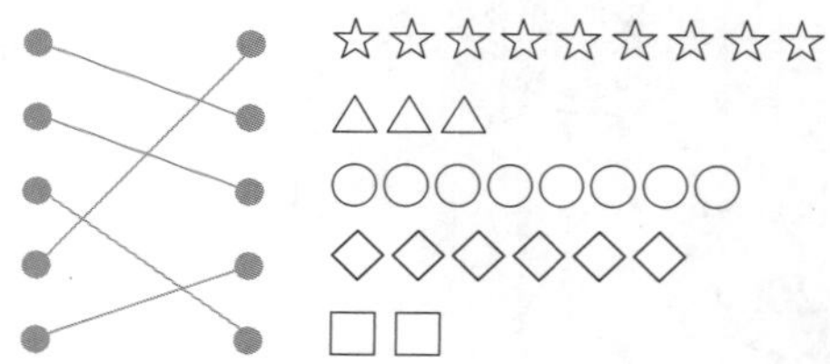

9. 10
10. 6
11. 2
12. 

13. 

14. 7; 9
15. 9; 7

Test Prep 7

1. C
2. B
3. A
4. D
5. D
6. 19
7. 9
8. 14
9. 11

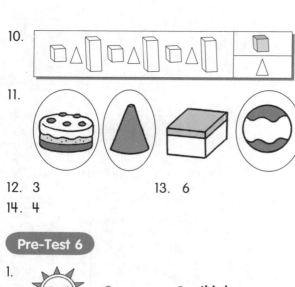

10.

17	16	13	12

greatest

11. Brad
12. Gina
13. Ella
14. 3
15. 7

Pre-Test 8

1. make
2. more than
3. add
4. less than
5. subtract
6. 9
7. 4
8. 7
9. 6
10. 2 + 3 = 5; 5
11. 9 – 4 = 5; 5

Test Prep 8

1. D
2. B
3. C
4. D
5. B
6. 5; 13
7. 7
8. 17; 8
9. 1
10. 13 ⊖ 3 = 9 ⊕ 1
11. 17 – 9 = 8; 8
12. 8 + 3 = 11; 11
    8 + 11 = 19; 19

Pre-Test 9

1. least
2. greatest
3. 4

Test Prep 9

1. B
2. C
3. C
4. D
5. B
6.

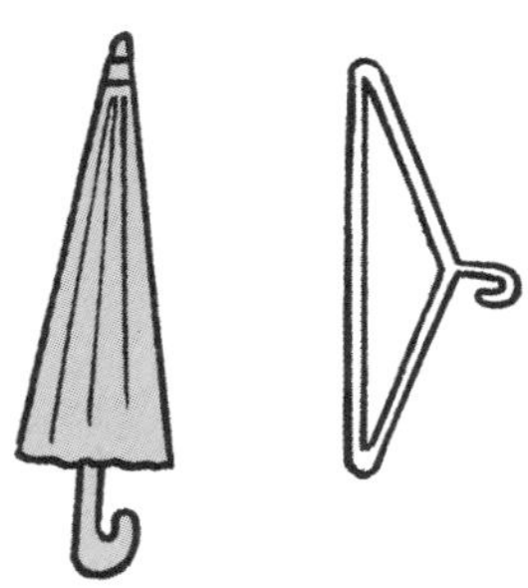

7.

8. B
9. 5
10. 12; 12; 2
11. 3
12. D
13. C
14. B
15. C

Mid-Year Test

1. D
2. A
3. A
4. D
5. A
6. C
7. A
8. A
9. B
10. D
11. D
12. D
13. B
14. D
15. A
16. D
17. C
18. C
19. A
20. B
21.

22. 9
23. 7
24. 2 3 4 7 9
25. 7
26. 6 + 3 = 9
27.

28. 8 – 2 = 6 OR 8 – 6 = 2
29.

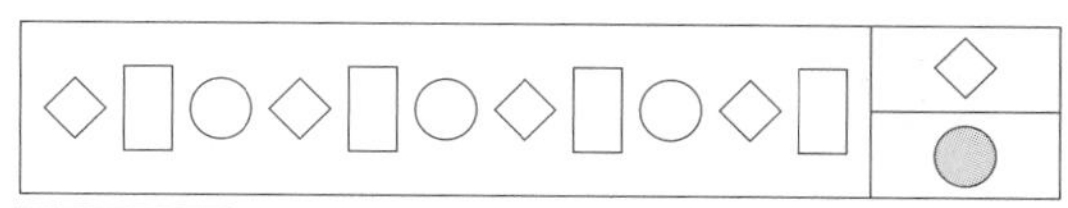

30.

31.

32.

33. twelve
34. 11
35.

11	13	14	19

least

36. 9
37. 8
38. 14
39. 9

40. 12
41. 5 + 3 = 8; 8
42. 10 – 8 = 2; 2
43. 11 + 3 = 14; 14
44. 19 – 11 = 8; 8
45. 12 – 5 = 7; 7

Bonus Questions

1.

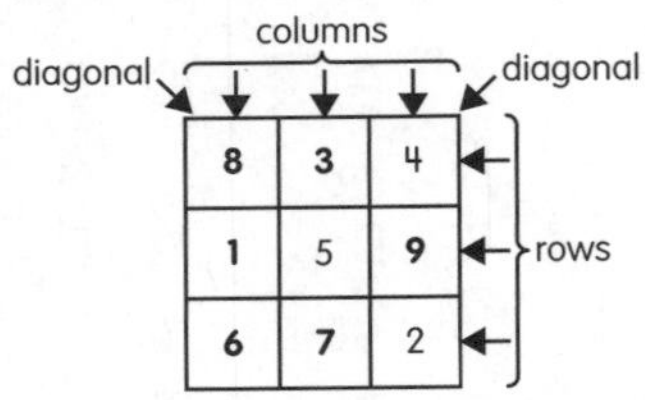

2.

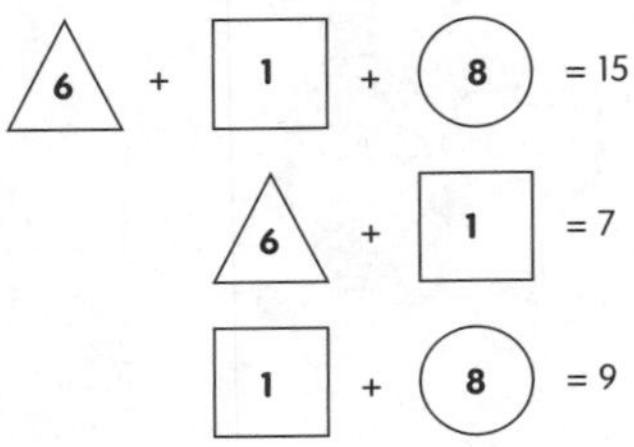

Pre-Test 10

1. lighter
2. heavier
3.

4.

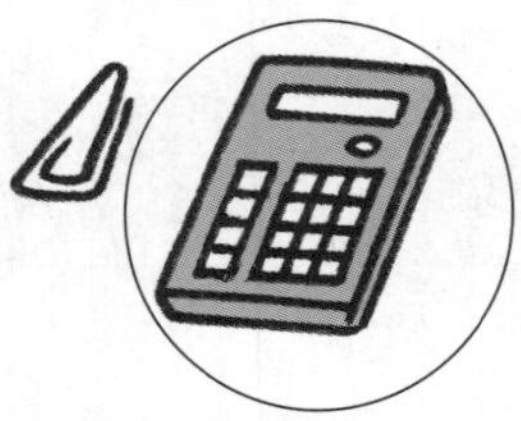

5.

6.

7. cup
8. cup
9. car
10. cup (lightest), table, car

Test Prep 10

1. B
2. D
3. D
4. A
5. C
6.

7. lighter
8. 3
9. book; apple
10. B
11. 2
12. 5
13. watermelon
14.

watermelon	papaya	mango	apple

heaviest

Pre-Test 11

1. more
2. fewer
3. same
4. 6
5. 8
6. 1
7. 7
8. 2
9. 1
10. erasers; rulers

Test Prep 11

1. A
2. D
3. D
4. B
5. A
6. Mike
7. 13
8. 4
9. 2
10. 12
11. 4
12. 3
13. February
14. 15
15. April

Pre-Test 12

1. less than
2. greater than
3. make
4. 14; fourteen
5. 11; eleven
6. 13; thirteen
7. 16; sixteen
8. 18; eighteen
9. 18
10. 10
11. 16
12. 13
13. 11, 13, <u>15</u>, 17, <u>19</u>
14. 20, <u>18</u>, 16, <u>14</u>, 12, 10, 8
15. 11
16. 19
17. 19
18. <u>11</u>, <u>15</u>, <u>19</u>
least

Test Prep 12

1. D
2. B
3. A
4. D
5. D
6. 39
7. forty
8. 3; 6
9. 23
10. 18, <u>20</u>, 22, <u>24</u>, 26, 28
11. 32
12. 26
13. 32
14.

18	**26**	**29**	**32**

least

Pre-Test 13

1. doubles fact
2. make
3. subtract
4. 13
5. 17
6. 12
7. 7
8. 9 + 5 = 14; 14
9. 12 – 3 = 9; 9

Test Prep 13

1. B
2. D
3. D
4. C
5. A
6. 33
7. 28
8. 9
9. 14
10. 15
11. 37 – 14 = 23; 23
12. 15 + 10 + 7 = 32; 32

Pre-Test 14

1. make
2. doubles facts
3. regroup
4. 8;
   2 + 6 = 8;
   8 – 6 = 2;
   8 – 2 = 6
5. 14
6. 26
7. 17
8. 26
9. 25 + 6 = 31; 31
10. 17 + 12 = 29; 29

Test Prep 14

1. D
2. D
3. B
4. C
5. D
6. 29
7. 38
8. 38
9. 22
10. 19
11. 29
12. 21

Pre-Test 15

1. week
2. time
3. morning
4. night
5. 4
6. 9
7. 1
8. 7
9.

Test Prep 15

1. D 2. A 3. B 4. C
5. B
6. 24 7. 4
8. 10 o'clock
9. half past 5
10. half past 11
11. 9
12. Wednesday
13. July
14. Winter

Benchmark Assessment 2

1. B 2. D 3. B 4. D
5. A 6. D 7. A 8. A
9. D 10. B
11. 3
12. dog; bricks
13. 16, 19, 22, <u>25</u>, <u>28</u>
14. Sunday
15. half past 7
16. 21 + 19 = 40
    There are 40 pages in the book.
17. 35 – 27 = 8
    She needs 8 more cards.
18. 40 19. 7
20. 10
21. 24 – 8 = 16
    Alex has 16 seashells.
22. 9 + 5 + 9 = 23
    Joe has 23 crayons at first.
23. 12
24. book 25. 16

Bonus Questions

1. C
2. $$\begin{array}{rcc} & \boxed{1} & 6 \\ + & 2 & \boxed{4} \\ \hline & 4 & 0 \end{array}$$
3. $$\begin{array}{rcc} & 3 & \boxed{0} \\ - & \boxed{1} & 7 \\ \hline & 1 & 3 \end{array}$$

Pre-Test 16

1. greater than 2. less than
3. make 4. twenty-seven
5. thirty-nine 6. 27
7. 29 8. 33
9. 28
10. 15, 19, 23, <u>27</u>, 31, <u>35</u>, 39
11. 38, <u>33</u>, 28, 23, <u>18</u>, 13, 8
12. 19
13. 32
14. 21
15. <u>19</u>, <u>21</u>, <u>25</u>, <u>32</u>
    least

Test Prep 16

1. C 2. B 3. C 4. D
5. D
6. 69 7. 59
8.

Tens	Ones
4	7

9. 86 10. 70 11. 49 12. 85
13. 68
14.

91	85	72	68	49

greatest

Pre-Test 17

1. counting on
2. regroup
3. count backward
4. 37 5. 23
6. 22 7. 26
8. 17
9. 18 + 6 = 24; 24
10. 25 – 18 = 7; 7

Test Prep 17

1. C 2. D 3. C 4. A
5. C
6. 9 7. 6
8. 17 9. 91
10. 69
11. 32 + 25 = 57; 57
12. 76 – 35 = 41; 41

Pre-Test 18

1. make
2. doubles fact
3. add
4. 16
5. 21
6. 16
7. 25
8. 2, 4, 6, 8, 10, 12, 14
9. 5, 10, 15, 20, 25, 30, 35
10. 10, 20, 30, 40, 50, 60
11. 4 + 4 = 8; 8
12. 9 + 9 = 18; 18

Test Prep 18

1. C 2. C 3. C 4. A
5. B
6. 3 fives = 5 + 5 + 5
   Sally has 15 apples in all.
7. 4 fours = 4 + 4 + 4 + 4
   The kittens have 16 legs in all.
8. 3
9. 3
10. 4
11. 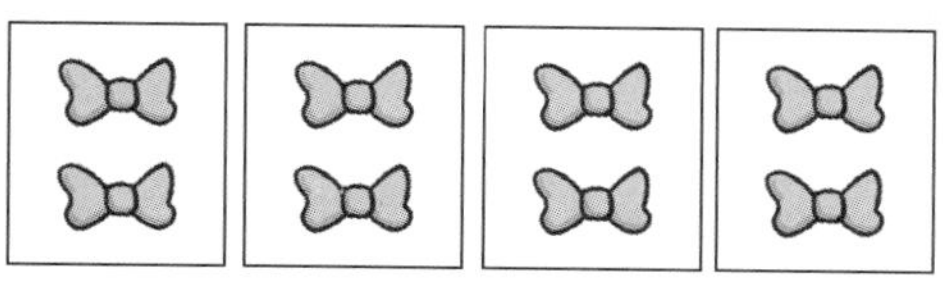
12. 3 + 3 + 3 + 3 = 12; 12

Pre-Test 19

1.
2.
3.

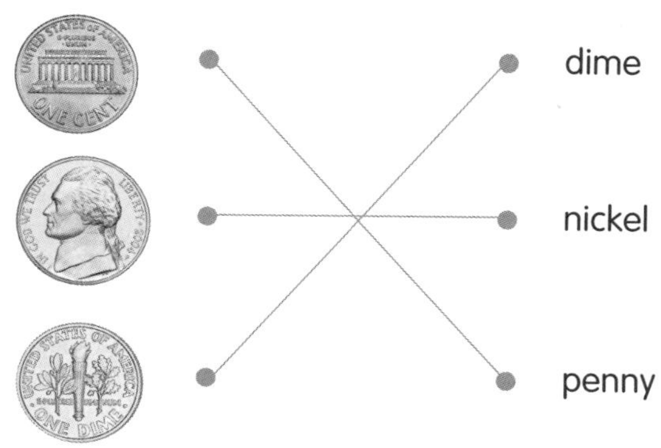

4. 2 5. 6 6. 15
7. 
8. 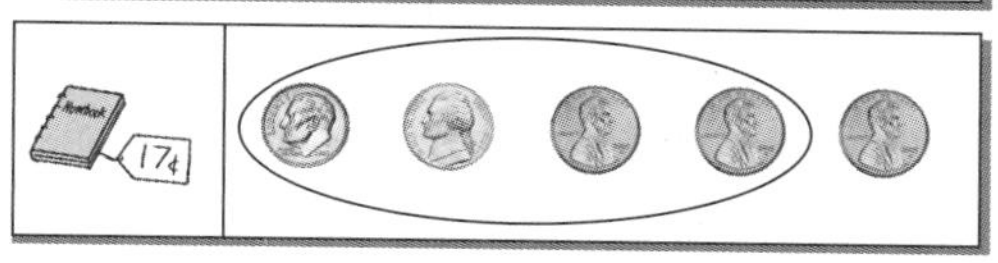

Test Prep 19

1. B 2. D 3. C 4. A
5. B
6. Answers vary.

7. 15
8. 5
9. 61
10. 5
11. 68¢ + 30¢ = 98¢
    She spent 98¢ for the two items.
12. 3

End-of-Year Test

1. B 2. C 3. C 4. D
5. D 6. B 7. A 8. A
9. C 10. C 11. A 12. A
13. D 14. B 15. B 16. D
17. C 18. D 19. A 20. C
21. 3

22. 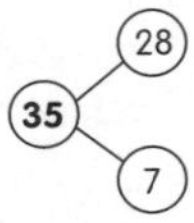

23. 5 + 3 = 8

24. 10

25. 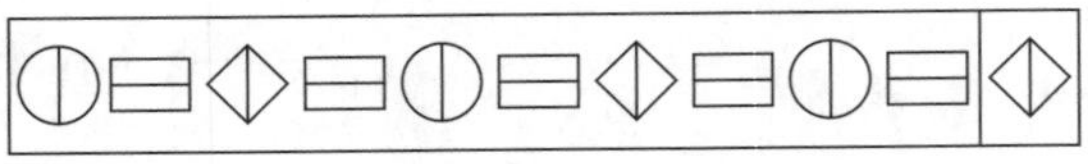

26. 

27. 17 OR seventeen

28. 6

29. 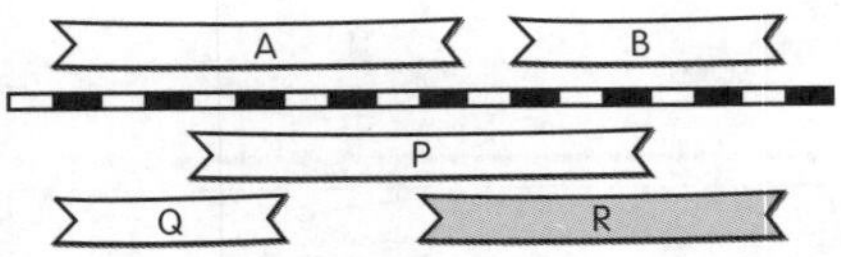

30. 6 31. 3 32. 35 33. 19

34. 61 35. 7 36. 4 37. 83

38. 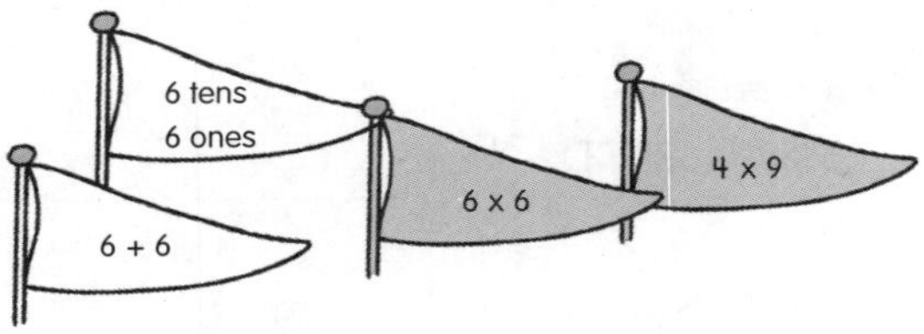

39. 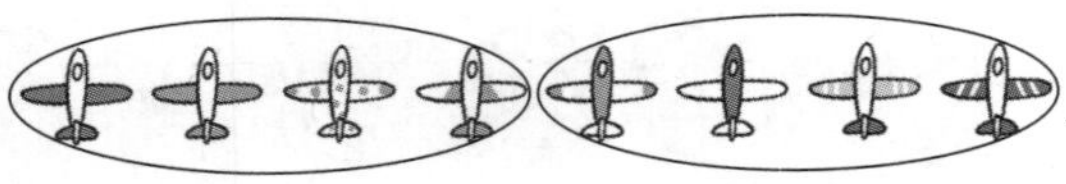

4

40. 15

41. 2 + 3 = 5
Sally had 5 hairclips at first.

42. 16 + 8 = 24
Bob has 24 stickers.

43. 40 – 22 = 18
18 more girls than boys are in the chair.

44. 35 + 29 = 64
Mrs. Walker has 64 beads in all.

45. 85¢ – 82¢ = 3¢
Gary has 3¢ left.

Bonus Questions

1.

	2	2
+	7	**8**
1	0	0

2.

	9	**3**
–	**3**	7
	5	6

3. Answers vary.

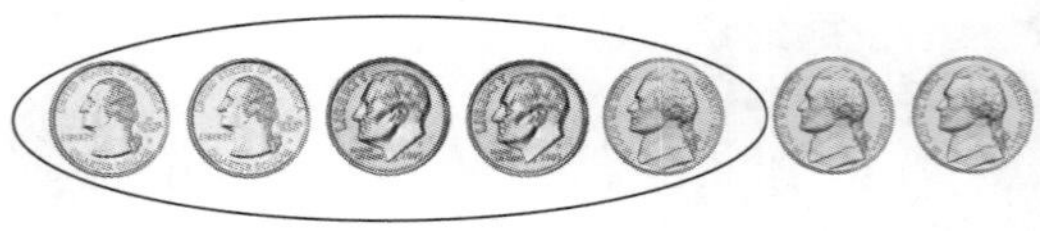

Name: ____________________

Math in Focus™

Student Record Sheet

Test	Date	Score	What I Need to Practice
Test Prep 1 Numbers to 10		25	
Test Prep 2 Number Bonds		25	
Test Prep 3 Addition Facts to 10		25	
Test Prep 4 Subtraction Facts to 10		25	
Benchmark Assessment 1 for Chapters 1 to 4		50	
Test Prep 5 Shapes and Patterns		25	
Test Prep 6 Ordinal Numbers and Position		25	
Test Prep 7 Numbers to 20		25	
Test Prep 8 Addition and Subtraction Facts to 20		25	
Test Prep 9 Length		25	
Mid-Year Test		100	

Name: ______________________________

Math in Focus™

Student Record Sheet

Test	Date	Score	What I Need to Practice
Test Prep 10 Weight		25	
Test Prep 11 Picture Graphs and Bar Graphs		25	
Test Prep 12 Numbers to 40		25	
Test Prep 13 Addition and Subtraction to 40		25	
Test Prep 14 Mental Math Strategies		25	
Test Prep 15 Calendar and Time		25	
Benchmark Assessment 2 for Chapters 10 to 15		50	
Test Prep 16 Numbers to 100		25	
Test Prep 17 Addition and Subtraction to 100		25	
Test Prep 18 Multiplication and Division		25	
Test Prep 19 Money		25	
End-of Year Test		100	